Michael Paramo may be identified as an asexual, aromantic, and agender queer Mexican-American in the Western world-view or, in another worldview, as Xicanx or simply human. Labels are not very important to them either way. Their relationship to the Earth has always held them together more than any assemblage of words. They love watching the bees go from flower to flower as they themselves stumble through life in the plastic, chemical, concrete wasteland of the modern colonial world, comforted by the mushrooms and microorganisms that will grow to break it all down. They say thank you to the old growth trees in the forest out of time that guided them and the ocean waves that washed the pain away.

Tightroping I
Wobble on horizons
Carved from modern ruin
Reach my hand out to the sun
The light at 'the end'
Reflects birth and death
Guts my vision
Punctures my breast
Stinging with possibility
Knowing that new life
Will grow from the pain

ENDING THE PURSUIT

Asexuality, Aromanticism &
Agender Identity

Michael Paramo

unbound

First published in 2024

Unbound
c/o TC Group, 6th Floor King's House, 9-10 Haymarket, London SW1Y 4BP
www.unbound.com

While every effort has been made to trace the owners of copyright material
reproduced herein, the publisher would like to apologise for any omissions and
will be pleased to incorporate missing acknowledgements in any further editions.

Unbound does not have any control over, or responsibility for, any third-party
websites referred to in this book. All internet addresses given in this book
were correct at the time of going to press. The author and publisher regret
any inconvenience caused if addresses have changed or sites have
ceased to exist, but can accept no responsibility for any such changes.

Typeset by Jouve (UK), Milton Keynes

A CIP record for this book is available from the British Library

ISBN 978-1-80018-285-1 (paperback)
ISBN 978-1-80018-286-8 (ebook)

Printed in Great Britain by Clays Ltd, Elcograf S.p.A.

1 3 5 7 9 8 6 4 2

With special thanks to Adi White for their generous
support as a patron of this book

Sponsors

Hannah Ackermans
Charlie Advincula
Diane Allan
Samantha Amenn
Ansso An
Carrie Anderson
Katherine Anthony
Stacy Archer
Abdul Asif
Haviva Avirom
Aren B
Kris B
Sophia B-V
Aleksandra
Baltrusaitis
Ricky Baribault
Rebekah Barker
Tóth Nóra Beatrix
Katie Bednara
Henry Behrens
Emily Belsito
Kat Berwick
Jay Besemer
Savanna Biedermann
John Bliss
Kiri Bo
Vera Bosch
Max Brasset
Daniel Budke
Andrea C
Zayn C.
Casey Carmody
Gina Carra

Mackenzie Carroll
Rowan Allen Case
Benjamin Chaim
Simone Chess
Chii
Kevin Chu
Hanna Cikovic
Jordi Civit
Kirsty Connor
Dean Conway
Rose Cooper
Kimberly Cortez
Jennifer Crawford
Allison Crisostomo
Nancy Crosby
Kate Cross
Mary R. Crumpton
Rachel Da Silva
Hervé Dago
Julia Daultry
Ignacio de Miguel
Díaz
Eavan
Dighton-Brown
Helen Doremus
Jeremy Edwards
Laura Edwards
Carolin Eichhorn
Elio
Elizabeth Elliott
El Epps
Noora Ervelius
David Eskinazi

EstanceDH
Ev
Finbarr Farragher
Ria Faustino
Zoe Feigen
Briar Fenn
Mathilde Fink
Clare Fitzgerald
Kaitlyn Flora
Iris Foxx
D Franklin
Cassandra French
Be Fritzson
Daniele Gibney
Ainsley Glaw
Aubrey Golpashin
Brian Gomoll
Annelise Gonzalez
Tyler Gray
Kailey Groat
Jason Gurevitch
Kenzie H
Lydia Hand
Rose Hardesty
Arwen Hargreaves
Nicky Harris
Freya Hausotte
Skylar Haynes
Kris Henges
Helmi Henkin
Robin Hill
Suz Hinton
Maria Högberg

Pandora Holcomb
Honour
Tiffany Hui
Teryhn Hurlburt
Emma Hutson
Daniela Illing
Jonatan Isakovic
Lu Jackson
Jennifer Jenkins
Alexis
  Johnson-Gresham
Charlie JP
Jack June
Caroline Keenan
M Kent
Leena Keränen
Phyllis Klarmann
Tanja Knoke
Matt Kremske
Kristin
Ren Kudo
Lisan Kuijper
Eli Landaverde
Tsy-Jon Lau
Ann Leslie
Benj Leung
Jennifer Levy
Lena Liedmeyer
Maddie Lim
Willem S. Lindal
Lioba
Liz@
  Anthropocene
  OnFire
Luke Yulian Löffler

Jay Logan
Lunakat805
Alyssa Machtmes
Karen D S Mackay
Siân Mackie
Björn Mahrt
Catt** Makin
Tony Manns
Lucie Marley
Anastasia
  Alekseevna
  Martemyanova
Sheri Martin
Cassidy Mayfield
Neir Mazur
Emily McCann
Elizabeth McClellan
Sarah McCoy
Cory McElrea
Scot McGregor
Frances McMullin
Alisa Merritt
Insa Miller
Lydia Milowski
Olivia Montoya
Jen Moore
Dylan Morris
Laura Morrison
Muhly
K. Nanthasarut
Aemia Narita
Melanie Nazelrod
Virat Nehru
Kes Nielsen
Noël

Tina Noon
Victoria Nordahn
Syksy Nygård
Robert O'Boyle
William
  O'Callaghan
Kelsey O'Regan
David Oakes
Anna-Maja Oléhn
Christian Ortiz
Alice Oseman
Christopher Pasillas
Lisa Perkins
Benjamin Perrett
Luke Pesch
Hilary Pittenger
Harrison Platt
The platypus
Tash Ploskodniak
Christina Potter
Katherine Quillin
Jennifer Quinn
V R
Willow R.
Nirina Rabeson
Rowan Ramona
Ann-Marie
  Ramsaroop
Stephanie Reasonda
Jynjer Rego
Sara Rhoades
Trish Roan
Ines Robin
Paul Robinson
Rhys Robinson

Ben Rocher

Kyle Roe

Lasse Rosenfeld

Cait Rottler

Emily Rushton

Elinor Sadowska

Bella Salazar

Blair Salzman

Tommy Samuel

Erin Sanders

Wells Lucas Santo

Justin Sauve

Jenni Schimmels

Ariana Schroeder

Peggy

Shannon-Baker

Shay

Amanda Leigh
  Sheard

Isobel Sheene

Bianca Shurey

Jennifer Sikes

Green Smith

Alex Stabler

Mary Stanfield

Emrys Stanton

Lucy-Anne Stanton

Richard Stevens

Sundas

Svenja

Nic Swann

Swantje

Felisha Thomas

Aivi Tran

Eva Ullrich

Sasha Valeria

Alex VanRooyen

Eris Varga

Éva Varga

Zéphyr Vaucher

Christa Ventresca

Margaret Verrico

Jo Violet

Robin Vodegel

Cici W.

Laurie Walker

Zach Walter

Alice Wang

Jerry Wang

Alice Warnet

Steph Wasek

Amaryllis Wayside

Jessica Weinberger

Jonas Wellingham

WesDirk

Wiechmänner

Kevin Wilson

Rebecca

Winters-King

Val Woodhouse

Ellen Woolf

Cass Zap

Lily Zhan

Alvin Zhang

Daniel Zura

Kayla Zuromski

This book is dedicated to my loving mother,
Martha Guillen-Paramo, and all of the people
who speak from their spirit, who speak truth in the world,
and who fight against the silencing and demobilizing spells
of fear. I love you.

"Don't chain yourself up inside any label,
your spirit knows exactly where to go. Our difficulty
is that we are assaulted constantly by noise and trivia."

Chrystos, 'Chrystos speaks at Creating Change 2011',
National LBTQ Task Force

Contents

Contents

Author's Note

As the editor of *AZE* journal (azejournal.com), a platform dedicated to publishing asexual, aromantic, and agender people's writing, poetry, and artwork, the experience of reading, editing, and publishing hundreds of submissions has developed my conceptual understanding of asexuality, aromanticism, and agender identity. Invested in amplifying the diverse perspectives of our communities, this experience motivated my approach in this book to cite the perspectives of asexual, aromantic, and agender people directly. This includes referencing works in *AZE*, online articles, and published research where we have expressed ourselves. This work has also been informed by hours of research parsing through online discussion threads. However, for privacy concerns, direct quotations and references to specific online discussions have been omitted. Instead, general references to trends that I recognized among these discussions are included, often signified by a vague reference or phrase akin to 'in online discussions . . .' This is most prevalent in Chapter 1, although can be found elsewhere in this book. Chapter 3 incorporates references to early online discussions from the 1990s and early 2000s. However, since these discussions are now only accessible via web archives and because of their importance to the historical record, they are sometimes directly quoted or referenced in this book.

Introduction

Like any creation, immaterial or material, a book is not an objective or neutral thing. It is a narrative, and each of us tells a different story. It is the diversity among us, informed by the contexts in which we grow up, unpredictable life circumstances, and a host of other variables that informs our stories. This variation among us is the true, yet too often neglected or villainized, beauty of humanity. I will now attempt to tell you a version of my story.

I have lived the overwhelming majority of my life in Orange County, California – an area of suburban sprawl built on the homelands of the Tongva, otherwise known as tovaangar. On these occupied lands, I grew up as a white-skinned Xicanx[1] in a middle-class Mexican-American family. I was acculturated into whiteness and directed to aspire to colonial (il)logics from a young age. My bilingual parents aspired for me to assimilate, so I was taught to speak English as a child. In my early adolescence, I became acquainted with my 'queerness,'[2] yet repressed these feelings as part of my Christian upbringing. This is not to say I was unloved, yet the ways in which I was different were simply not recognized or celebrated by my family or the surrounding 'community' I grew up in. This led me to feel ashamed of myself for much of my adolescence and early adult life. In my late teens and early twenties, I came to realize that I also did not experience sexual or romantic attraction nor was I interested in forming any such relationship built on these feelings. I grew similarly distant from the expectations of what it meant to be a 'man.'

While for a short period in my adolescence I pondered whether to repress myself and assume a life of conformity, I understood that this would be impossible. I simply could not stomach such a 'fake' existence wrapped in a constant pursuit of some false sense of security or unfulfilling 'success' that did not speak to me.

From a young age, I was told that I was curious and creative. I used to be somewhat obsessed with fact-based books and lists of information about the world. It was through obsessively browsing this information, both offline and online, that I learned much about people and places that I never would have been exposed to in the Western classroom. This exploration was a privilege and blessing that fueled my natural curiosity. It was through this process that I began to think about the world more critically.

After the social terrors of attending public school as a queer Xicanx student, I matriculated at California State University, Fullerton (CSUF) and eventually stumbled upon the field of American Studies late into my time as an undergraduate. It was here that I encountered educators who grappled with many uncomfortable truths that I had been ignorantly shielded from in my youth. It was around this time that I became acquainted with the term *asexual* through a Google search. Quickly identifying with the term myself, I realized that there was a lack of discussion surrounding asexual people's experiences and expressions. This absence encouraged me to launch *The Asexual* journal in October 2016 as a platform to publish a host of asexual perspectives in the form of writing and art-work. The journal went on to publish its first issue early the following year.

Soon after completing my undergrad, I enrolled in the master's program in American Studies at CSUF. I came across theoretical works such as Michel Foucault's *The History of Sexuality, Volume 1* and Judith Butler's *Bodies That Matter* that shaped my perceptions of gender and sexuality, as well as other fields. More and more I realized the now obvious con-clusion that things hadn't always been *this way* nor did they have to continue to be.

Shortly before completing my master's, I experienced a strong 'mental shaking' that could be summarized as an unex-pected confrontation with my mortality. Although I had dealt with depression and social anxiety for many years, this event sent me into an anxiety that I had never experienced before. Every day became a deep struggle; an internal war. In this vulnerable place, I contended with the reality that, as the late Lee Maracle stated, I was an "upright *homo sapien*" in a chaotic, unpredictable, and interconnected world who had the responsibility to learn how to walk in this life.[3]

It was this 'mental shaking' that led me to seek out others who spoke from a grounded perspective.[4] Listening to these voices helped me find the confidence to reestablish my per-sonhood and worldview external to the modern Western colonial model and trajectory. Artmaking became a tool to stabilize myself. I wrote poems, created digital self-portraits, and produced music that led me to reflect and learn in new ways. These lessons informed my concept of ending the pur-suit, or otherwise divesting from and refusing to reproduce separable ways of seeing and being in the world.

This is when my understanding of interconnectedness, the

idea that everything is connected to everything, both in the material and immaterial sense, re-emerged in my life. I say re-emerged because, as a child, it did not occur to me to separate or draw lines where nature did not draw them. I did not see myself as disconnected from the land around me; I touched and played with the Earth. The act of communicating with others was not bogged down with separateness, distance, or strictly performative interaction. The differences between myself and others did not seem important, nor did they separate us into hierarchies of 'superior' to 'inferior' or 'normal' to 'abnormal.' Therefore, I came to recognize that I had been taught to internalize the separable worldview as truth.

As my worldview developed, I continued to manage *The Asexual* journal. Although the journal was initially created to address the general lack of understanding surrounding asexuality and asexual identity, I soon recognized that asexuality intersected with other topics in ways that were not deeply explored. This encouraged me to publish journal issues on themes of the body, race, sex, representation, pride, attraction, and self-discovery. The journal went on to publish issues dedicated to agender and aromantic perspectives. The continued growth of the journal on social media, its recognition by external sources, and its explorations into various topics was encouraging.

After being accepted into the Institute for Gender, Race, Sexuality & Social Justice at the University of British Columbia, located on the occupied territories of the Musqueam people, I learned to think more critically from a decolonial perspective. Through this experience, I made connections with my work on asexual, aromantic, and agender identity.[5] Influenced by queer and decolonial theory, I changed the journal's name from *The Asexual* to *AZE* to expand its focus and include ace (asexual), aro (aromantic), and agender writers and artists. The name reflected what I began to loosely frame as *azeness*, or the experiences of 'absence' that are shared by asexual, aromantic, and agender people amidst the norms and expectations of colonial cisheteropatriarchy.[6]

I soon learned that the separable way of seeing had produced the 'masculine world' of division and hierarchy,[7] which placed the 'rational' European man as the pinnacle human subject who holds the authority to subjugate, exploit, and objectify 'irrational' and 'inferior' Others.[8] I would later find that recent scientific endeavors in quantum theory had illustrated that the Western worldview's foundation on separability and compartmentalization was being recognized by modern Western scientists as inaccurate and unfounded. This was identified by theoretical physicist David Bohm, who wrote:

> The classical idea of the separability of the world into distinct but interacting parts is no longer valid or relevant. Rather, we have to regard the universe as an undivided and unbroken whole. Division into particles, or into particles and fields, is only a crude abstraction and approximation. Thus, we come to an order that is radically different from that of Galileo and Newton – the order of undivided wholeness.[9]

The beginnings of an epistemological convergence between what have been broadly categorized as Western and Indigenous ways of knowing showed me how interconnectedness was transcending worldviews that colonizers once placed in diametrical opposition to one another, framing the Indigenous as irrational regressive uncivilized object and the Western as rational progressive civilized subject.[10] In other words, "scientists, physicists, philosophers, and academics [were only now] coming to terms with views long held by indigenous peoples."[11]

Around this time, I became more assured in orienting myself toward decolonial consciousness. I understood that our memories of interconnectedness had been assaulted in an effort to assimilate us into colonial-capitalist structures because "without a collective memory, communities are easily absorbed and privatized."[12] Growing up in a post-apocalyptic world where day-to-day life functioned as if genocide and land dispossession across Turtle Island and Abya Yala[13] never occurred, I questioned: Why was it 'acceptable,' as if it had been encoded in society, to forget and devalue Indigenous peoples' lives and ways of knowing as not worthy of active consideration in our lives?

This was an issue within queer discourses, where I found that colonialism was rarely discussed. This silence has been identified as a larger issue within the academic field of queer studies, where there have been calls to not just acknowledge Indigenous peoples, but to develop "a consciousness about the ongoing colonial reality in which all of us living in settler colonial states are entrenched."[14] This is something I also hope to contribute with this book by demonstrating how many of the dominant ideas we may have about sex, romance, attraction, and gender are informed by colonial narratives. Essential to this work is de-threading ideas that have been woven into our daily lives by the colonial needle.

This is easier said than done, since the colonial fantasy narratives we have been taught to adopt have been made to be difficult to identify, critique, and dismantle. Sociologist Silvia Cusicanqui reflected on how spoken or written language, for example, is used by the colonial apparatus to conceal truth rather than identify it.[15] This is especially true when considering how

Indigenous languages were fiercely targeted everywhere in favor of colonial or European languages. This linguistic dimension of colonialism has significantly lessened the languages we as humanity collectively use (and value) to make sense of reality. Additionally, when we are actively discouraged from and blocked by barriers that impede truthful conversations toward action, the consequences of this silence manifest on a personal, communal, and species-level scale. Settler colonial nations are invested in using words to *separate* themselves from the genocides and gross forms of exploitation they are built upon,[16] which includes using them to symbolically 'reconcile' on their own terms without taking actual steps to decolonize.[17]

This disjointed way of framing things was privileged in the modern colonial world and obscured the power of interconnected thinking. Learning this lesson has informed how *Ending the Pursuit* is written; functioning as both an artistic autoethnographic and a theoretical academic work, this book takes an interconnected approach to analyzing and reflecting on deeply personal subject matter – identity, behavior, relationality, performance. It is also inspired by the process of intuitive writing, or of finding the words by listening to one's intuition rather than being constrained by dominant expectations of what writing should be.[18] It was not only written to represent transformation, but to initiate it.

Some people may initially look at a book reflecting on asexuality, aromanticism, and agenderness and ask *What does this have to do with decolonization?* or *Why is colonialism relevant to this discussion?* This is because these subjects are interconnected and inform one another, despite often not being put in conversation – they cannot be separated without missing what is to be gained from seeing them simultaneously. Part of the purpose of writing this book is to cultivate our endurance to make connections between concepts that may initially seem abstract, fragmented, or disconnected.

Transformational possibilities may unfold when we see how things that may seem separate are actually entwined together: how we see ourselves, how we see each other, how we see the world, and how we act in it are all subject to change. This book represents just one such possibility in its application of decolonial thought to asexuality, aromanticism, and agender identity. It offers insights into (re)claiming our personhood by departing from the pursuits of conforming to what has been demarcated for our lives and our futures.

Through writing this book I was drawn to be more self-reflective and enveloped in a process of personal growth and survival. This meant engaging in the day-to-day work of becoming more assured in my voice while navigating life. Sometimes I struggled to keep writing, while at other times I found writing helpful to feel some sense of groundedness. Like anything and everything, the process has been transformative.

Words are not my friends
They are my fingers extending
To dimensions I will never know
They are my flawed symbols
My hardened failures
My attempts to grasp
At what it was I felt
While I was here

Coming Out of the Impossible

I can only describe the process of *coming out* as heaving up words – words that felt too minimal to capture what it meant to describe myself. I have never found it easy to communicate with people who have been conditioned to adopt the cisheteropatriarchal lens as truth. Even if I am not outright rejected for being 'queer,' always feeling like I am on the outside has meant that navigating everyday life is fraught with challenges others may never encounter. Many of the obstacles I face as a queer person are as a result of how others have been conditioned to think about 'people like me.'

Throughout over 500 years of colonialism, what became called *queerness* was construed as abnormal, so that revealing one's divergence from cisheteropatriarchal norms was viewed as a social transgression. This created the conditions for *coming out* to become a recognized social ritual, where the 'queer' who had been, in many cases, first outcasted from the circle of humanity by colonial cisheteropatriarchy was now tasked with the pursuit of acceptance or at least social toleration for their own safety, health, and wellbeing. Rahul Rao describes coming out as "an attempt to reconcile a divided self" amidst oppressive conditions where "the structure of secrecy and disclosure at work presupposes the existence of something called 'sexuality' that describes an aspect of a hidden interiority that we think of as the 'self.'"[1] The very existence of the social ritual of coming out illuminates how the modern colonial world is defined by silence and violence.

The elongated form of the phrase, *coming out of the closet*, reflects an emergence from a closed, confined, and concealed metaphysical space defined by torturous silence and inner anguish. It implies that a sort of beneficial transference may occur when an individual enters into an improved space of openness where those who are already socially accepted exist by default. How often do you hear of a person coming out as heterosexual? Or coming out as someone who experiences sexual attraction or who desires to form a romantic relationship? Or coming out as a cisgender man or woman? Almost never. Therefore, there is a (sub)conscious awareness of how cisheteropatriarchy ostracizes individuals who are problematized by its very institution. Coming out is often an attempt to quell or lessen chronic psychological distress, dysphoria, or lack of understanding caused by the naturalization of colonial queerphobia.

For asexual, aromantic, or agender people, coming out is less likely to produce reactions of outright approval or disapproval than it is to provoke confusion or disbelief at the mere existence of such an identity. This is because each of these concepts challenge fundamental ideas related to cisheteropatriarchy: (1) the naturalized belief that all human beings experience sexual attraction and desire,[2] (2) that all human beings experience romantic desire and should form coupled relationships built on 'romantic love,' (3) that all human beings inherently have a gender within the binary of man or woman. Asexual, aromantic, and agender people are tasked with justifying ourselves because, in one sense or another, we are viewed as impossible. Given how deeply embedded these beliefs are, I have found that the people who we reveal our identities to often embark on a pursuit to find a 'real' reason for our identities rather than to accept the uncomfortable possibilities that asexuality, aromanticism, and agenderness create. This pursuit to find an explanation that satisfies them may involve observation, interrogation, and other measures. Ending the pursuit here would mean admitting that asexuality, aromanticism, and agender identity are *possible*, which would in turn challenge how sexuality, romance, gender, and attraction are commonly understood. This would expand our beliefs about what it means to be human and to open up how we see the world.

Under whose eyes
Am I defined
Separated
From rotting flesh
And dreams of difference
With whose mouth
Has our possibility been consumed
Yet incubating still
In the belly of that beast
That has bitten more of us off
Than it can chew

Conditional Identities

As I grew older and it became more evident to others around me that I was not interested in finding a (hetero)sexual and (hetero)romantic partner – failing to fulfill the expectations of cisheteropatriarchal masculinity – people began to credit my sexual, romantic, and gender differences to some internal abnormality or deficiency. Was it because my hormones were imbalanced? Was it because I was mentally disabled? Was it because I was socially awkward and had never given sex a try? Was it because I was afraid of romantic commitment? Was it because of a parenting failure? Had I not been taught gender roles properly?

My body became the scientific experiment of other people's dissection. I am reminded of the time I was questioned whether my body was physically normal for a man and if I should be medically examined to verify if there was an alleged 'deeper issue' going on. I could blame the individual people for asking such questions, for engaging in pursuits to rationalize my identity through the locus of the cisheteropatriarchal worldview, but this would miss the root cause of the issue. This is because, in many cases, people have internalized certain narratives and beliefs as truths that have gone without critique until moments of confrontation. Coming out is one such confrontation, where the person on the receiving end may believe the asexual, aromantic, or agender person to be impossible, unnatural, or in need of correction.

Asexual, aromantic, and agender people are commonly subject to the task of educating people to deconstruct internalized narratives about sex, romance, gender, and life in general when we come out. Some people who desire to cling to the perspective that asexuality, aromanticism, and agenderness are unnatural, broken, or somehow in need of correction and bury the possibilities that these identities unearth. This can take many forms, which largely revolve around making our identities conditional or otherwise dependent on some 'deeper problem.' The following is a non-exhaustive list of different 'conditions' that are commonly imposed upon asexual, aromantic, and agender people when we come out. It deconstructs many of those narratives commonly cited by asexual, aromantic, and agender people and demonstrates some of the overlapping ways in which we experience invalidation – relegated to the realm of impossibility.

'Attention seeking' (asexual, aromantic, and agender)

Perhaps the most basic way in which asexual, aromantic, and agender identities are made conditional next to flat-out denial is to frame them as attention seeking, or as a joke not worthy of further consideration. Rather than as useful communicative tools to convey one's experiences, this narrative misconstrues our identities as being products of selfish behavior. This attempts to frame asexual, aromantic, and agender people as nothing more than desperate and self-serving.

There are many challenges to discussing our identities openly because of this narrative. This is especially true online, with discussion threads, social media posts, and blog entries noting how others have claimed things such as 'you're just looking for attention' or 'stop trying to act like you're special.' Being the creator of a platform dedicated to publishing asexual, aromantic, and agender voices, I am familiar with how narratives such as these are used in an attempt to delegitimize and silence conversations about our identities. This speaks to the challenges of being 'out' online. Although we are not coming out to the entire internet when we simply talk about our experiences online, we are always open to receiving these types of invalidating responses from people insisting that we are only talking about our experiences for attention.

This narrative has also been used to discredit calls for inclusion. This is because the unknown and misunderstood status of asexual, aromantic, and agender identities can make them easy targets to sell an anti-inclusion narrative to an uninformed population. For example, after the city council of Yarra, Australia decided to fly the aromantic flag in 2021 for Aromantic Awareness Week, this was met with outrage from a few vocal opponents, who used the event to profess a reactionary political agenda. One newspaper article characterized it as "nothing more than vacuous, attention-seeking, victim playing and narcissistic emoting" that was "pushing a far-left radical agenda."[3] This response demonstrates how symbolic acts of asexual, aromantic, and agender awareness may be used to characterize those who accept their legitimacy as 'crazy' or irrational to stoke social anxieties over inclusion. Furthermore, mischaracterizing acts of symbolic recognition as 'far left' rather than as more in-line with liberal representational politics is a discursive move to frame 'leftist' perspectives as disingenuous, out of touch, and self-absorbed. Symbols of inclusion such as flags and even identity terminology can thus become sites of political contention that may be used by some people to push reactionary narratives.

Accusations of attention seeking are also hurled at agender people, often under the dominant belief that any gender identity outside of the binary is disingenuous and thus should be subjected to scrutiny. In an article for *Teen Vogue*, Mya, an agender interviewee, poignantly stated: "We are viewed as these teenagers on the internet making up labels and being too 'sensitive,' despite the fact that there have always been people who existed outside of the gender binary, in all cultures, in all time periods."[4] This interconnected perspective speaks to the gender variance that is inherent to humanity across space and

time. As such, it recognizes cisheteropatriarchy as the imposition that has made gender variance appear 'unnatural' and thus
demonstrates the shallow and ahistorical basis that claims of
attention seeking are based on.

Shy or socially awkward (asexual and aromantic)

In 2017, I participated in a video compilation discussing asexuality for Buzzfeed LGBT. After the video was published, I
noticed a comment directed at my appearance left as a response
on a social media platform. The comment stated: "that
Michael P is cute, so it can't be that they can't find anyone to
bone them. Maybe they're just super nervous or something."
Although encountering these types of comments are minor
events in my life, they have collectively told me a deeper story
and inspired me to think about what undergirds people's
words – what were their presumptions; what were they pursuing? Because this person perceived me as sexually attractive,
they did not attribute my asexual identity to being unattractive or sexually unwanted, but rather to self-discomfort.
Witnessing how my asexual identity was attributed to being
"super nervous or something," connected my experience to a
larger trend of asexuality and aromanticism being framed as
by-products of shyness and social awkwardness.

This narrative can become internalized by many aces and
aros, who might ask themselves whether they have misinter-
preted their own shyness or social anxiety as asexuality or
aromanticism. Some aces and aros have indicated how this
narrative has created self-doubt in their lives that has negatively impacted their wellbeing. Narratives such as 'Aromantics
are afraid of commitment' can similarly contribute to negative feelings being internalized, leading to self-questioning
and feeling like one is in need of 'correction.'[5] For aces and

aros who do already have an aversion to dating or relationships (not all aces and aros do), this can send us down a rabbit
hole of thinking we are just afraid to be sexual or romantic,
rather than that we do not experience sexual or romantic
attraction.

I have witnessed various online discussions of aces and aros
doubting whether their identities are a mask for their anxieties
because of invalidating narratives such as this. Some aces and
aros have deconstructed this dilemma by identifying how their
lack of attraction is not in conflict with their social anxieties.
This was explained in a post for the September 2015 Carnival
of Aces, in which the author noted: "If that were the case, the
attraction would be there and would be fighting the anxiety.
There's never been a situation where I've thought, 'I'd like to
get with that girl, but I'm too afraid to talk to her.'"[6] However, for others it may be difficult to pinpoint our feelings and
understand where they may be rooted, since there are many
overlapping layers to parse through. This is especially because
of the erasure of asexuality and aromanticism amidst narratives that devalue our experiences as conditional.

Some aces and aros have noted how this idea that they are
just shy or have social anxiety is both asserted and internalized on the premise that they can and should 'correct' their
social behavior to 'overcome' their identity. The presumption is that if we 'put ourselves out there' enough, especially
in contexts where doing so is seen as normal, we will stop
being asexual and aromantic. This was commented on by
Jessica Vazquez in an article for Autostraddle: "I just thought
I was too awkward or shy when it came to dating. I attributed my aversion to nightclubs and casual hookups to my
social anxiety."[7] These sexual and romantic social expectations can encourage some aces and aros to try to persevere

through social behaviors and acts that make them feel broken to try to pursue what is positioned by the dominant society as 'normal.'

a person who assumes
an asexual to be without
what they consider to be
life's purpose
its greatest joy
of sucking, emitting, receiving, penetrating
they frame it as my negative
to be beyond an asexual's reach
so that we never will compare
to their pleasure's peak
and that we must only be left
in the trenches of
some pitiful nightmare
but it is then again, i wonder
what their imagination has left
missing
in those who see me
missing
in those that hold onto
missing
to see life from another
missing
angle, i wonder for them
for their possibility maybe
as they wonder for me
briefly holding stasis
i vanish in the wonder
full

Not having 'tried it' (asexual and aromantic)

Several years ago, I enrolled in a class on the topic of exploring sexualities from a sociological perspective. Late into the semester, I came out to the class when the subject of asexuality emerged in a lecture session. We were examining the Kinsey Scale: a system of categorizing sexuality on a scale from heterosexual to homosexual devised by Alfred Kinsey and first published in 1948. Kinsey had included a mark for individuals who could not be classified on his scale, and the professor asked if anyone knew how these individuals were labeled. I responded by stating that they could be considered 'asexual.' The professor confirmed that the X on Kinsey's scale represented what may be considered asexuality. Kinsey himself actually classified these individuals as people who had "no socio-sexual contacts or reactions," which differs from the lack of sexual attraction. At the time, however, I saw my asexual identity as equated with a lack of sexual desire, or a general lack of sexual interest, rather than a lack of sexual attraction, or a lack of attraction to a person based on a desire for sexual contact with them.

As stated by scholar Justin J. Lehmiller, "the Kinsey X classification emphasized a lack of sexual behavior, whereas the modern definition of asexuality emphasizes a lack of sexual attraction."[8] After this discussion point was made, I stated that I identified as asexual. This seemed to garner some surprised reactions, but the discussion moved on until the end of the class session. After the lecture ended, one student enquired if they could ask me about my asexual identity. Having come out a few times before, I was aware of the risks of this, yet accepted their request. I was met with the question: 'If you haven't had sex, how do you know you're asexual?'

This type of question is a common response to asexual and aromantic coming-out experiences. Rather than accept that asexual or aromantic identity may be legitimate, a person might advise or insist that one should try sex or romance first before they identify as asexual or aromantic. This narrative may be directed toward a person who has never been in a long-term sexual or romantic relationship based on the assumption that when they 'try it', it will inspire sexual and romantic feelings within them that were previously not present. Asexual people who have had sex, as well as aromantic people who have been in romantic relationships, exist and have not suddenly stopped being asexual or aromantic. A person who denies the possibility of asexuality or aromanticism on this premise may then either ignore such occurrences completely or argue that the asexual and aromantic people who have 'tried it' and still identify as asexual or aromantic have simply not had sex or been in a romantic relationship with 'the right person.' This was acknowledged in an article for Feminism in India by Meghna Mehra in regard to asexuality, who wrote: "If any asexual individual has had sex before, they are further gaslighted by being told that maybe they had bad sex and they should try to have sex with someone else/more often."[9]

There are various ways in which this narrative has been countered by aces and aros, such as reversing it back to the source. For instance, in an article for BBC News, Jenni Goodchild wrote: "Well if you're straight have you tried having sex with somebody you know of the same sex as you? How do you know you wouldn't enjoy that?"[10] Rather than reverse this narrative, Jade Nicole flips it in her aptly titled piece 'Find the Right Person' published on *AZE* in 2018, noting that this idea of the 'right person' is not universal since everyone has a different relationship to love, making the 'right person' someone who is willing to love you for you, not for themselves.[11]

'Giving up' on relationship formation (asexual and aromantic)

Several years ago I came out as both gay and asexual to someone in my family who I was told was accepting of gay people. I assumed this would mean that they would accept my gay asexual identity. When I came out as gay, I was welcomed openly. They expressed how happy they were for me. There was excitement in their eyes and they seemed eager to support me. However, when I revealed that I was also asexual, their excitement vanished almost immediately. Their feelings of happiness quickly changed to concern. They told me 'not to give up,' believing my asexuality to be a confession that I had surrendered the pursuit of a relationship. I attempted to explain that I was *actually* asexual, but they did not appear too comfortable sitting with that reality. Instead, their sympathetic attitude toward me took over our conversation. My asexual identity transformed me into an object of pity in their eyes, rather than as someone to connect with on equal terms. As the curtains closed on our conversation, I was left wondering: *Why did they interpret my coming out to be my way of telling them I had given up on something I had no interest in pursuing?*

It was as if my asexual identity somehow meant that I had lost out on the possibility to achieve 'liberation' from the confines of the closet. This is because sex is sometimes regarded as a pathway toward achieving liberation from states of repression. In one of the earliest articles written from an asexual perspective, Myra T. Johnson's 'Asexual and Autoerotic Women: Two Invisible Groups,' published in *The Sexually Oppressed* in 1977, she described how these groups of women "have been oppressed by a societal consensus that they, as free and unique individuals, do not exist." Johnson argued that asexual women were rendered invisible in the 'sexual revolution' of the 1960s that established liberation in sexual terms: "Not fitting this popular definition of 'liberated,' the asexual woman seems to only rarely receive recognition in feature articles or staff written columns."[12] Positioning women's liberation in sexual terms meant excluding asexual women who did not conform to the popular image of what it meant to be 'free.' Johnson's essay begs the question: If liberation can only be imagined in sexual terms, where does this leave asexual people?

This assumption that asexuality is symptomatic of 'giving up' on finding a life partner makes the identity seem like a personal 'problem'; a cover-up for a presumed inability or failure to form a relationship, which, in many people's minds, should be the cause of embarrassment or pity. As described by scholars Luke Brunning and Natasha McKeever, asexuality is equated in the mainstream imagination with "a pitiful existence," meaning that when asexual people come out they may encounter "people [who] demand an explanation as to why, feel sorry for them, and hope that they change their minds so that they can experience sex." This may be coupled with the assumption that the asexual person in question has recently ended a tumultuous relationship, that they need to keep searching until they find someone, or that they are simply fearful of relationship formation.[13] This frames asexual identity as a phase or, as described by Mark Carrigan, "a quirk of their present state rather than a significant and enduring feature."[14] This is how coming out as asexual can become interpreted as an admission of defeat – a confession of ending one's pursuit of what every 'normal' person is supposed to seek in life.

Aromantic people endure similar accusations that coming out is conceding to a life without love or purpose in the absence of romantic relationship formation. Romantic expectations are inherently connected to sexual expectations, since romance without sex (and vice versa) is not viewed as satisfactory enough toward achieving fulfilling relationships or a healthy life. Aromantic people have identified how this presumption can originate from the (hetero)romantic expectation that women should pursue their 'Prince Charming,' or a man who will 'complete' them, and that men should, to some extent, express some interest in forming a relationship with a woman (although with far less social pressure than women). Yasmin Benoit spoke to how this narrative has been reinforced in mainstream media narratives and can quickly become imposed onto audiences:

> In a world where we were encouraged to envision ourselves as our favorite Disney princess, finding a Prince Charming was the crescendo of our story – in our dreams and in reality. I didn't have a problem with this until I realised there was a genuine expectation for me to partake in this behaviour and not doing so was seen as abnormal.[15]

These fairytales and fantasy narratives about romance push people, particularly young girls, to meet the gendered expectations of romantic love. "To my young mind, that was how things were supposed to be [. . .] I lived in the belief that one day a prince would come and rescue me," wrote Namrata K for Feminism in India.[16] This results in the assumption that coming out as aromantic is not only 'impossible,' but an admission of a failure to fulfill the normalized pursuit of romantic relationship formation.

romance
bored me
like a routine
the idea of it
too organized
but i could see
how others organized
their thoughts
toward my 'loveless' life
and it made me consider
what resided
in that blank space
in me
where romance
'should' be?
if i didn't yearn
for another half
was i
a (w)hole?

'Secretly gay' (asexual)

Since asexuality is viewed as an impossibility, it is sometimes folded into the narrative that it is a cover-up for being gay, which itself is defined through sexual attraction.[17] There is a parallel here with how bisexual identity is sometimes socially framed, since when an individual comes out as bisexual their identity may be delegitimized as either a stepping stone to gayness or as a way to 'soften the blow' of coming out as gay. Scholar Nikki Hayfield connects this to the "binary understandings [that] have dominated within Western cultures."[18]

Being gay and asexual is also viewed as an impossible contradiction because gayness is often hypersexualized. This was noted in a virtual discussion for the journal *Psychology & Sexuality* by Randi Gressgård: "Some would perhaps argue that an asexual sexual orientation is like meatballs without meat and that being gay and asexual is a contradiction in terms."[19] C. J. Bishop reflected on this element of the conversation:

> Additional confounds observed relate to the comments that some individuals may identify as a 'gay asexual man.' This concept seems counterintuitive in the sense that for one to identify as 'gay,' he is admitting an attraction to members of his own sex. That is not to say that this distinction is an error or somehow incorrect; however, the current literature is lacking the means to bring understanding to someone identifying in this way.[20]

This comment reveals how *attraction* is commonly framed as an entirely sexual experience. Understanding attraction as multilayered might open the possibilities for gay asexual experiences to be understood more widely, as other expressions of attraction become recognized outside of the shadow of sexual assumptions (more on this in Chapter 2).

Immaturity (asexual, aromantic, and agender)

For asexual and aromantic people, the immaturity narrative is rooted in the belief that forming a sexual and romantic relationship is an essential part of growing up. This infantilizes asexual and aromantic people, with the presumption being that they are a 'late bloomer' who will eventually mature out of identifying as asexual or aromantic. Aces and aros may begin to hear this narrative directed toward them during their adolescence, since this is when sexual and romantic expectations begin to become more prominent. For agender people, the immaturity narrative is entwined with the idea that gender nonconformity is a phenomenon reserved for young people who simply 'need to grow up.' The presumption here is that becoming a man or a woman as it is defined under cisheteropatriarchy is an essential part of adulthood.

There are many online posts discussing how the immaturity narrative takes shape. Many of these discussions have been initiated by asexual, aromantic, and agender people who have reflected on their experiences encountering others who have treated them as immature for their age or trapped in a stage of underdevelopment. These experiences can frequently result in self-doubt, as evidenced by these discussion threads often posing the question of whether others have experienced similar scenarios in their lives or if they have also doubted whether they are, for instance, 'asexual or just refusing to grow up,' 'aromantic or childish,' or if their agender identity is just a result of being 'too young to know.' These accusations that their identities are merely by-products of youthful immaturity may be leveraged by many others, from peers and parents to therapists, who have substantial influence in shaping one's self-perceptions.

The claim that there is a general absence of asexual, aromantic, and agender people of 'mature age' may also be used in an attempt to reinforce the immaturity narrative. For example, this was highlighted in an interview article for Ace Week in 2021 by The Ace and Aro Advocacy Project, which opened with the description that "older asexual people are often invisible and many don't even realize they exist."[21] A 45-year-old interviewee for the article stated: "I'd love for allo[22] folks to stop assuming I'm ace simply because I'm older and my hormones are out of whack."[23] The identities of older aces may be discredited based on their age, aligned with the common assumption that older people, especially older women, are 'already' asexual.[24] This contributes another dimension to age-related invalidation narratives, making the asexual person either 'too young to know they're asexual' or 'too old to be sexual anyways.' In online discussions, aromantic people beyond their adolescence have similarly spoken of being made to feel immature for not being interested in romantic relationship formation – so much so that they may prefer not to come out for fear of being looked down upon. Agender people in their thirties and beyond have similarly reflected on 'feeling old' in comparison to the agender community in online discussions. These dimensions reflect how there might be no accepted age in which asexual, aromantic, and agender people can simply just *be*.

To deconstruct such narratives, it appears necessary to destabilize this notion of *maturity* and what constitutes its representation, since the metrics that are commonly used to demarcate who is 'mature' and 'immature' are often socially entwined with one's progression toward reproducing cisheteropatriarchal formations. It is also important to note that there are asexual, aromantic, and agender people who may come to realize that they no longer associate with the label as they age. These cases may appear disruptive since they can be interpreted as 'affirming' the invalidating narratives directed at communities who are attempting to disentangle their identities from such claims. However, rather than ignore this complexity, simultaneously recognizing such cases blurs the either/or binaries and affirms that there is nuance to all of our experiences.[25] The acknowledgement that our journey through identities can be fluid is important, not to reinforce invalidation narratives (especially since this application is not merely limited to asexual, aromantic, and agender identities), but to remind ourselves that we are not obligated to commit ourselves to words that, for better or worse, categorize our own and each other's experiences.

Sexual assault or trauma (asexual and aromantic)

The idea that asexuality and aromanticism are by-products of sexual assault or other traumatic events is a relatively common assumption that can be imposed onto asexual and aromantic people even if they have never been sexually assaulted. In these cases, family members and peers may question or impose that a certain traumatic event was the origin of an asexual or aromantic person's identity. In these cases, trauma may be used as a device to denounce the existence of asexuality and aromanticism by freezing the person in a space of pity that reinforces the idea that sex and romance are the keys to a fulfilling life – a life that aces and aros have allegedly been locked out of by traumatic events. Scholar Eunjung Kim identified that this narrative has been promoted by authoritative voices, including medical and professional experts, who act as intermediaries for audiences while speaking over the people themselves. Kim cited the case of a sex therapist brought onto a US television show in 2006 who denied that asexuality could exist without such cause: "maybe something to do with trauma, or abuse, or repression, or severe religiosity that has predisposed you to shutting down the possibilities of being sexually engaged."[26]

There are, however, aces and aros who have experienced sexual assault or other traumatic events and intracommunally understand how their identity may be interrelated with their trauma. This subject has been discussed among aces and aros in various online discussion forums, who sometimes question whether their asexual or aromantic identity is rooted in trauma. However, some critics have pointed out

that recognizing these conversations may be seen as risky or
avoided because of the fear that they reinforce the stereotype
that asexuality or aromanticism are merely by-products of
trauma. Academic researchers may neglect this topic "to
avoid the implication that these events may be a cause of
one's asexuality or to potentially pathologize asexuality in
any way."[27]

While not all asexual and aromantic people who have
experienced sexual assault understand their identity in this
way, some aces and aros who have experienced sexual assault
have discussed how their trauma from these events changed
their feelings, attitudes, and attractions toward others sexually and romantically. In either case, imposing this narrative
onto aces and aros or insisting that we must be ace or aro
because of our trauma from the outside can cause further
harm. Such an imposition can make aces and aros feel that
they should try to engage in certain behaviors that they think
will 'correct' them, especially when under the pressure of
others. This can take many harmful forms, including *corrective
rape*, where "the victim explains that they are asexual, and the
assaulter wants to 'show' the victims that they are wrong"
with the narrative being that they can 'fix them.'[28]

With romance's inherent sexual attachments and its necessity in regard to ideas of 'love' in the mainstream imagination,
aromantic people may be read as 'emotionless' or even 'socio-
pathic' (sometimes with the assumption that this is because of
trauma) when coming out, which can lead to being coerced
into toxic dynamics to avoid further ostracization and harassment.[29] As explained by Steph Farnsworth in an interview
with *Cosmopolitan*: "Erasure isn't a privilege, and it causes
long term mental health issues which we can't get support
for. There are also real dangers of abuse, hatred, sexual assault,

harassment, and/or stalking."[30] Aromantic people must often therefore work against these assumptions that their identity is inherently a by-product of trauma amidst further trauma-causing threats when coming out.

Of course, how aces and aros understand their identity can vary considerably. Such an understanding, that one's identity is connected to one's trauma, may frustrate or discomfort people who are working to disentangle such associations. The nuance here is to recognize the importance of deconstructing the idea that asexual and aromantic identity are *inherently* connected to trauma. However, such nuance is often not easily conveyed or accepted, especially with uninformed social attitudes and media portrayals reinforcing dominant tropes. Some have advised that such acknowledgements are therefore best reserved for intra-communal conversations.

Disability (asexual, aromantic, and agender)

That asexual, aromantic, and agender identities are by-products of a disability is one of the most pervasive narratives rooted in the way disabled people are perceived under cisheteropatriarchy. This has many dimensions because of the range of experiences and social assumptions pertaining to different disabilities, which can also overlap. The imposition of this narrative can include questions about hormone levels, neurodivergence, physical ability, and more. Eunjung Kim argues that "disabled adults are desexualized and infantilized," which renders their sexual orientation irrelevant and causes their participation in "heteronormative institutions such as marriage and parenting" to be understood as "unusually triumphant – to the same degree as it is forbidden."[31] Paul Chappell similarly identifies that "youth with disabilities are typically constructed as de-gendered and as asexual" due to misconceptions held by the non-disabled community.[32] Furthermore, Lindokuhle Ubisi explains that "socio-medical discourses portray disabled individuals as infertile, non-sexual, and degendered" and reinforce this characterization as truth.[33] Disabled people who are also asexual, aromantic, or agender are therefore made invisible and excluded from the possibility of forming a 'successful' relationship because they are always already desexualized, deromanticized, and degendered in the dominant imagination.

This creates complex challenges when coming out. For disabled aces, this may mean being perceived as an obstacle to deconstructing narratives that are imposed onto disabled communities. An anonymous disabled ace writer commented: "as a disabled person I am part of a community that is constantly fighting to be seen as sexual beings, to throw off the shackles of the very same loaded label with which I choose to identify. Where does that leave me?"[34] Courtney Lane wrote in an article for Ace Week that since "an enormous amount of disability activism revolves around fighting to be seen as a sexual being," this can contribute to "blanket statements such as, 'Yes, ALL disabled people have and enjoy sex, because we're human just like you . . .'" becoming common. At the same time, ace discourses also attempt to separate themselves from disability in order to appear 'normal' to the dominant culture. Lane remarked that these intracommunal narratives exist "to make ourselves seem more palatable to outsiders," but that they can do "real, tangible harm to members of the community who live at these intersections."[35]

In a personal essay reflecting on their experiences of being asexual and disabled, Charli Clement wrote that the assumption that asexual people are inherently disabled along with the assumption that disabled people are inherently asexual urged them to conceal their identity in late adolescence: "I should be able to claim my asexuality, and my disabled identity, whilst being able to challenge the misconceptions that my communities face. I shouldn't have to pick between my identities, but I fear it is something I will always have to cautiously balance."[36] Coming out as a disabled ace therefore requires not only navigating the dominant assumption that one is only asexual because one is disabled, but also the intracommunal narratives that seek to separate asexuality from disability and disability from asexuality. In response, Courtney Lane created Disabled Ace Day in 2021 to open space for the voices of disabled aces to be recognized, rather than silenced.[37]

Disabled aros encounter similarly complex issues when confronting identity navigation. This was discussed in an interview by The Ace and Aro Advocacy Project with disabled and neurodivergent aros, where many spoke of how their aromanticism was entwined with their disability. Some spoke about being unsure, while others disagreed that their aromanticism and disability were interrelated. Similar to disabled aces, some interviewees indicated how their aromanticism was claimed by others to be conditional on their disability even when they themselves rejected this association. One aroace[38] interviewee noted how making aromanticism and asexuality conditional on disability may be done out of a pursuit to settle discomfort: "I think to some extent they're relieved I'm aroace, because for a lot of abled people who don't realise they're ableist, it's uncomfortable to imagine an autistic cane-user being romantic and kissing people or having sex."[39]

This mentality frames different coming-out experiences for disabled aros, who have explained how coming out to neurotypical and non-disabled people differs from coming out to neurodivergent and disabled people. For instance, interviewee Mars expressed how coming out to fellow autistic people is more comfortable on the basis that "we are deeply aware that there is more to the human experience than the societal rules imposed on us, and as such I feel like we're less likely to impose those same rules on each other," in comparison to neurotypical people who may be more dismissive of difference from social norms. Other interviewees similarly expressed that disabled people were generally more accepting and understanding with coming-out experiences than non-disabled people.[40]

People who identify outside of the Western gender binary are commonly portrayed as disabled as a way to simultaneously 'rationalize' and inferiorize their existence. This has been a longstanding practice in Western medical institutions, with evidence dating back centuries. "One of the prevailing myths that exists, even within the medical community, is that gender identity is a mental disorder," states a 2019 article for the website of US healthcare provider HCA Virginia.[41] This association is what led the fifth edition of the *Diagnostic and Statistical Manual of Mental Disorders* in the US to assert that "gender non-conformity is not in itself a mental disorder," changing the categorization from 'gender identity disorder' to 'gender dysphoria' in 2013. Yet, diagnostic categories continue to be seen as a stigmatizing force, even as they may "preserve access to gender transition-related health care,"[42] which makes navigating such issues challenging, given how the medical industry functions in the modern colonial world.

The legacy of pathologizing gender nonconformity continues to be used to reinforce the allegedly 'scientific' basis of cisheteropatriarchy, despite the fact that many cultures across space and time have had and continue to have gender-diverse and non-cisheteropatriarchal social formations even after or amidst hundreds of years of colonial violence, gendercide, and assimilation (more on this in Chapter 6).[43] Agender people therefore may still face opposition when coming out because of the presumption that their identity reflects a disorder. This pathologization can further result in negative effects on health and wellbeing, which is reflected in the medical classification of gender dysphoria. Similar to disabled aces and aros, disabled agender people are erased, with their agenderness being viewed as an inherent reflection of a disability and vice versa.

Blocking desirability (asexual and aromantic)

When a person who is gauged to be desirable comes out as asexual and aromantic, their identity may be invalidated as an obstacle that blocks a person who desires access to their body. Desirability is primarily measured by one's sexual desirability as determined through the modern colonial gaze. This often goes unspoken, yet determines many of the commonplace assumptions regarding who is dominantly deemed to be 'attractive.' Desirability can also relate to a person's potential to fulfill the role of being a partner in a long-term romantic relationship. This is because, as demonstrated by a 2015 study's assertion, there is a common belief that "choosing and attracting the right romantic partner are two of the most critical challenges in human life" because of the perception that "romantic partners also influence the survival and success of any children we might have, through the care they provide and the heritable qualities they pass on."[44]

Relationship formation glued together by romance with the outcome of reproduction is upheld as an essential life pathway. José Esteban Muñoz reflected on this perception, noting how queer people who "do not choose to be biologically reproductive [. . .] are, within the dominant culture, [perceived as] people without a future."[45] Because of how dominant and universal this attitude is presumed to be, it can lead to an 'attractive' person's asexual and aromantic identity being interpreted as a false claim to not engage in the 'necessary' acts of sex and reproduction. This may result in various forms of emotional, psychological, and physical violence directed toward asexual and aromantic people in an attempt to 'correct' them to overcome what is interpreted as a false obstacle.

This can vary for aces and aros depending on their experiences within the hierarchies of ableism, homophobia, sexism, transphobia, and white supremacy, since these forces permeate every facet of modern colonial life and inform who is generally deemed desirable. In an academic review of gender, race, and asexuality, the authors noted that "Black bodies are often viewed as untouchable, either promiscuous or unattractive; Asian bodies are often viewed as uniformly feminized and submissive; Brown bodies are often exoticized," each assumption of which affects racialized asexual and aromantic people differently.[46] Asexual women of color are subject to sexual objectification through patriarchal racialized fetishization, which can invalidate their identity differently from white asexual women. In an article for Affinity, author Anais Rivero included quotes from asexual women of color on how this can intersect with their experiences. In one account, an asexual Latina woman reflected:

I had to listen to a lot of guys say disgusting stuff because of my body type. Besides that, my friends used to say to me that I could 'have any man I wanted' and often asked me why

wouldn't I have sex with anyone. I thought there was something really wrong with me.[47]

Her reflection illustrates how she experienced sexualization
simply because of the way her body was interpreted. The
sexual expectations exerted upon her body by the dominant
gaze led her to question whether she was 'broken' as a result
of not conforming to sexualized narratives. A Black asexual
woman similarly reflected:

> It took way too long to feel right with myself though because
> the only black women I ever saw on TV were extremely sex-
> ualized and exoticized. [. . .] I am totally fine with never
> getting married or being in a romantic relationship [. . .] I've
> been able to accept myself and understand my feelings fully.[48]

These women's reflections illustrate the challenges of navigating asexual identity under racialized fetishization as women
of color in the modern colonial world.

This can especially invalidate the identity of ace women of
color as being less 'possible' than white ace women. This was
commented on by one participant in a 2019 study, who noted
that "any minority is different . . . And face it, people are
always going to be a lot more accepting of a White asexual
than they are of a Black asexual, especially since minorities are
over- sexualized, period."[49] A 2018 *AZE* article entitled "'You're
Such a Waste': Too Attractive to be Asexual" by Danyi also
reflected:

> When I first started identifying as asexual, one of the reasons
> I wasn't believed, especially in the case of men, was because
> of how my body was seen as attractive. The first time I was

told I couldn't be asexual was because it would be a waste of
my pretty face and nice body. [. . .] To him, because I don't
allow people to touch me and enjoy my body physically, I'm
a waste of a person.[50]

Aces and aros who are perceived as attractive may be interpreted as a 'waste' because their identity disrupts the servicing
of desirability, which is disproportionately skewed through
the cisheteropatriarchal gaze.

This conditional narrative predicated on the assumption
that asexual identity is a 'false' refusal of sexual engagement
can, as previously mentioned, lead to *corrective rape*, most often
against ace women by men who view asexual identity as a
sexual 'challenge.' Despite asexual oppression often being
erased, corrective rape occurs under the guise of 'fixing' or
'awakening' sexual attraction in aces.[51] Other manipulative
behaviors may be used to socially pressure aces to conform to
sexual expectations placed upon them, which can be reinforced through the internalization of one's own identity as a
deficiency that can be overcome.

These pressures may also be applied to aros, who can be
made to feel obligated to conform to the expectations of
romance and romantic relationships that they are desired
within. In online discussions, some aros reflected on being
made to feel 'self-centered' or rude after rejecting the romantic attraction of others by expressing that they are aromantic.
This generally arises from their identity being viewed as an
attempt to block another person's romantic interest, rather
than as a legitimate expression of self. Deconstructing feelings
of selfishness, guilt, or shame can help lessen the internalization of social pressures that emerge simply from being aro or
ace in a romantic or sexual world. Melissa reflected on this

from an asexual perspective in an article for *AZE*: "I don't recall any particularly dramatic shift in my thinking or any epiphany that roused me from my self-loathing; it was only a small, quiet miracle of self-acceptance and the gradual shedding of shame."[52]

Do I want to look 'sexy' or is beautiful to me
What 'sexy' is to others
Is the look in my eye a lure
For bodily stimulation
Fill me up with the vapid joy of affirmation
That I make you feel sexual attraction
Cast the spell on you that fails on me
Immune to the pull, am I the fool
Or you to decide what I am doing

Excusing undesirability (asexual and aromantic)

If a person is perceived as unattractive, coming out as asexual and aromantic may be interpreted as an attempt to deflect their undesirability. In the context of asexuality, scholar Sarah E. S. Sinwell commented on the relationship between asexual identity and desirability in media representation, noting that popular media frequently depicts or otherwise signals to the audience that a character is asexual based on their lack of compliance with "cultural codes of desirability." Qualities such as "fatness, disability, Asian-ness, and nerdiness, for instance, have all been associated with asexuality." Asexual characters are coded as asexual for the audience not because "they do not experience sexual attraction, but rather because they are not sexually *attractive*."[53] What is perceived as a sign of asexuality to audiences then is commonly skewed through the lens of desirability. As a result, when aces and aros who are viewed as unattractive or undesirable come out, their identity may simply be viewed by others as an attempt to excuse their status as undesirable.

Several years ago, I wrote an article explaining how I had internalized self-hatred over my body image that made me feel like I was unattractive and therefore socially worthless, which demonstrated the confluence of undesirability and a lack of self-worth in my body. I remember at one time having a fear that coming out as asexual would be attributed to my (presumed) undesirability, that people would credit my identity to being a way for me to excuse my inability to find someone who would be attracted to my body. Some aces in online discussions have echoed similar sentiments, noting their fears over others crediting their identity to their 'unattractiveness' or 'never finding someone who is attracted to them anyways' when coming out. This accusation of course arises out of the presumption that everyone inherently seeks to be in a sexual and romantic relationship, and thus any claim that is interpreted as opting out from this pursuit must be spurious.

Asexuality and aromanticism may not only be read as a cover for one's undesirability, but also as a marker of undesirability itself. When I have come out as asexual or aromantic, people have viewed me less desirably, seeing me as a less viable potential partner. In one case, someone who once expressed their interest in me, knowing that I identified as asexual, changed their perception when I expressed to them that I also identified as aromantic. It seemed my aromantic identity evaporated most of the desire they had directed toward me. My status became unattainable or simply unattractive, since I was no longer perceived as being able to reciprocate the romantic desires they sought from a relationship. The hope that mutual romantic love could be the cornerstone of a healthy relationship in the absence of sex was the proverbial nail in the coffin, it seemed.

In general, there is the misperception that aromantic and asexual identity means being totally without any feeling or emotion at all. As a 2020 article on WebMD stated, "A common myth is that aromantic people, especially aromantic asexual people, are cold and robotic."[54] Aromantic people themselves have expressed how their identity causes others to perceive them as devoid of emotion or "heartless"[55] or as "cold and logical robots."[56] This perception of aromantic identity generally alters how desirable aromantic people are viewed to be under the dominant gaze when they come out. While pushing back against the assumption that aros and aces are emotionless is important to deconstruct this stereotype, aros and aces also are not obligated to endlessly pursue validation from dominant social perceptions.

Hang over my head
That I am not beautiful
Enough, or sexy
Enough, or attractive
Enough, to allure
An other to make me
Whole, I suppose
That is a 'normative'
Supposition
For the tainted
Imagination
But has it ever occurred to you
That I am beyond
The grasp

Of rotten cores
Immune to the pull
Of your mind
Has it ever occurred to you
That I am floating free
Suspended in a place
I can call
My own?

Embracing the Impossible

As this chapter has reflected on from different angles, coming
out as asexual, aromantic, and agender commonly results in
one's identity being treated as *conditional*. Asexual, aromantic, and agender people may avoid coming out simply to
offset the work and energy that frequently accompanies it as
a result of their identities being viewed as impossible. To
address this, awareness campaigns – Agender Pride Day (May
19), Aromantic Spectrum Awareness Week (February 21–27),
and Asexual Awareness Week or Ace Week (the last full
week in October) – and educational resources have taken up
the task to attempt to offset this work. One guide to being
inclusive of asexual students noted:

> Your lack of knowledge can make asexual students feel unim-
> portant. Worse yet, it can make them wary of coming out or
> living authentically. So, be prepared. Understand the basics
> of asexuality so that no student has to go through the emo-
> tional labor of explaining it to you.[57]

In an article for The Body Is Not An Apology, Dawy

Rkasnuam noted for others to "keep in mind the emotional labor you're asking for, and be sure to make the effort to learn about asexuality and aromanticism yourself" rather than basing reactions on limited assumptions.[58] As stated on AUREA, a resource hub for aromantic people, "When it comes to aromanticism you will rarely, if ever, come across people outside the LGBTQIA+ community who know what you're talking about," so "be prepared to explain what being aromantic means to you and have some resources handy for further reading."[59] Some agender people in online discussions noted that the emotional labor required when coming out (which is often followed by rejection) is often so intense that they would rather just routinely be misgendered.

However, asexual, aromantic, and agender people will continue to face challenges with acceptance because to embrace their identities requires expanding the dominant worldview of what is possible and deconstructing fundamental beliefs of cisheteropatriarchy. The pursuit to make asexuality, aromanticism, and agenderness conditional seems to ultimately stem from the deeply rooted recognition, whether conscious or not, that how the West has organized, structured, and policed sex, romance, and gender is 'normal' and 'natural.' It is a refusal to accept that cisheteropatriarchy and the 'science' it is based upon could possibly be wrong; that its institutionalized formation could be destructive and divisive for humanity rather than beneficial and generative.[60]

my my my
i love every body
i will love every body
that will feel my decaying skin

i wonder what they will think
of my body
will they care
that i didn't have sex
or had no romantic relationship
or that my gender was so 'queer'
i'll ask the ants that crawl on my back
and the maggots that eat my flesh
pulling my heart to pieces
if my body
nourishes life
like any body
did
and in the silence
of useless rhetoric
and their glorious feast
i'll tell them
i love them too

Because sex, romance, and gender constructs are so essential to the modern colonial world's assertions of what it means to be human, such an unconditional embrace of asexuality, aromanticism, and agenderness opens up how we see ourselves as a species. However, rather than flat-out reject the premise that asexual, aromantic, and agender identity can be conditional, another part of embracing the 'impossible' includes acknowledging that multiple things can be both true and false at the same time; that, for instance, these identities can be understood as conditional for some people while not for others. This is not to reinforce dominant narratives, but to leave space for people to forge their own interconnected understandings. This may discomfort us, but it is exactly this discomfort that invites us to embrace the impossible plurality of existence; that we can be both different from each other, yet the same – "imagine difference without separability," as described by Denise Ferreira da Silva.[61]

Part of my intention behind opening *Ending the Pursuit* with a discussion on worldviews and interconnectedness was to emphasize that the Western framework is only one way of seeing the world. So why should we reinforce the ways in which it divides us into factions of 'normal' and 'abnormal'? Why should we pursue understanding the world only through this lens and condition others to do so as well? These questions are posed to generate a reflection on what we know and how we know it to encourage us to embrace what it means to exist in the world.

We cannot flee from the impossible, nor should we ignore it in pursuit of a simpler illusion. As Avery Gordon wrote, "Life is complicated." While this phrase may be dismissed as cliché, Gordon asserted that it is "perhaps the most important theoretical statement of our time" for the way it illuminates how each of our lives are "simultaneously straightforward and full of enormously subtle meaning."[62] Amidst it all, I am becoming acquainted more each day with embracing the *impossible* complexity of reality – with appreciating and learning to *be* in the stream of life – and in this process I invite others to do so as well.

I am not pure or tainted
What I believe cannot be conflated
Into a binary or flawed model
That requires chopping me up
Into beautiful pieces of stardust
Why should I be invested

In convincing you that part of complexity
Is how my existence is 'different' from yours
Yet also 'the same,' that lines are horizons
Of possibility breaking
Deep in the fog
Of this colonial war
The unattainable terra nullius
Undiscovered, unclaimed
Suns setting, shadows enclosing
When the dust settles
Who are you to know me
Being haunted by possibility
Clarity is fleeting
Sometimes it feels like if I am still
Not in a pursuit, I might collapse
But in moments of weakness I keep steady
Attracting the light that keeps possibility
Burning

2

ATTRACTION

There is a social power of attraction, the way it presents itself in the atmosphere of social interactions. In the dominant Western worldview, the word *attraction* is most often used to refer to two people coming together to form a cisheteropatriarchal coupling defined by mutual sexual attraction and signified by romantic love. The expectation that everyone experiences (hetero)sexual and, therefore, (hetero)romantic attraction has led to our behaviors constantly being 'read' through the cisheteropatriarchal lens, which has restricted when and how we feel comfortable expressing ourselves.[1]

Dominant understandings of attraction are rooted in Western 'scientific' discourses that ascended through the burgeoning colonial world alongside eugenics. Sexology emerged as a new "science aimed at discovering the laws of sexuality" in the nineteenth century[2] to regulate populations in service of European colonial agendas. This is the origin of the modern field of *sexuality*.[3]

[This field of knowledge] spread beyond Western centres, as policy-makers and intellectuals in [so-called] New World nations, as well as in African and Asian colonies and empires,

were well versed in the latest scientific theories and were concerned about the design of a healthy, productive population[4]

The global proliferation of sexuality as a field of study deeply
shaped ideas about how sex, romance, gender, and attraction
were 'supposed' to function. This was part of the global
dissemination of cisheteropatriarchy, which included the
exportation of the view of women as naturally submissive and
intellectually inferior, the inferiorized category of homosexuality and, subsequently, homophobia,[5] and the 'scientific'
persecution of people who did not conform to the gender
binary.[6] The global institutionalization of cisheteropatriarchy
first occurred through waves of colonial military, religious,
and political authorities who fundamentally altered the life-
ways of Indigenous peoples, including their expressions of
'gender' and 'sexuality.' Scholars have noted various targets,
including "the Muslim model of sexually-knowing, assertive
women;"[7] "the generally more tolerant indigenous attitudes to
homosexuality [in pre-colonial Indonesia];"[8] the proliferation
of "same-sex eroticism in many, perhaps all, of the indigenous
societies of Latin America;"[9] and the non-heteronormative
notions of binary gender and sexuality in "West Africa, South
Asia, Polynesia, and what are now known as 'the Americas.'"[10]
While the older rhetoric of missionaries and military men
marked such expressions for elimination on the basis of them
being unholy or "demonic,"[11] sexologists added another layer
to this, ensuring that colonial cisheteropatriarchy was now
"stamped with the imprimatur of [Western] science."[12]

Colonialism was framed by European colonizers as a
cleansing force that allegedly rid the world of "the abomin-
able degradation of many indigenous peoples and the extent
to which the devil had tricked the people into the most

horrific and gruesome acts."[13] On the gender and sexual side, this 'cleansing' was carried out through the direct violence, social and religious terror, and the enshrinement of Western sexological discourses in colonial structures. This included the infamous Section 377 of the British penal code, which criminalized "carnal intercourse against the order of nature" and was used as a model throughout the British Empire after first being implemented in British India in 1860.[14] Colonial empires used legal structures and social indoctrination to impose cisheteropatriarchy and the productive model of the nuclear family. The legacies of ongoing colonialism continue to deeply shape our worldviews today, which includes how we understand, express, and value attraction.

Within person-to-person relationships, attraction remains primarily interpreted through the Western concept of *sexual orientation*. This has not only determined how one's attraction is understood in regard to the gender binary,[15] but has instituted a categorical system by which everyone is organized based on their sexual object of interest or attraction, even if they would rather not be.

The prioritization of the sexual reveals itself in the following hypothetical: if a man were to say 'I'm gay,' the vast majority of people would define this as 'he wants to have sex with men' and not 'he wants to be in a romantic relationship with a man that isn't sexual' or 'he wants to be in a sensual relationship with a man that isn't sexual or romantic.' The reason this perception is overwhelmingly common is because sex is prioritized in the Western worldview as the primary manifestation of attraction. Sexual attraction is not assumed to be a mere possibility, but as inherently present.

For those of us who find ourselves outside of the 'sex equals attraction' worldview, our expressions of person-to-person attraction tend to be devalued, disbelieved, infantilized, and reduced because they are not socially intelligible or valued. This is why asexuality and aromanticism are often misdefined in the popular imagination as 'having no attraction.' Under this limited and limiting perspective of attraction, expressions that stray from mutual (hetero)sexual and (hetero) romantic attraction – qualities that are deemed to be necessary for the formation and maintenance of 'healthy' and 'productive' relationships – are consistently devalued.

When sex is treated as attraction's ultimate expression, the true complexity of attraction and its potential will always be obscured and devalued by the shadow of sex. In the shadows, we are only able to engage in various forms of intimacy, such as romantic displays of affection, platonic friendships, sensual touch, or emotional and intellectual connection, for what has been regarded as the underlying goal: to *pursue* sex, to *claim* sex, to *feel* sex. But what can happen when we begin to *pull apart* this dominant framing of attraction and open spaces between the lines that have been drawn?

Suspended in a space, the void
Is like being in another dimension, simultaneously
Our eyes gaze through the li(n)es
Floating in chaos, but with beauty all around
I am the quazar
I eat the walls that divide us
Consuming the shit feeds my body
Embodying the so-called blackhole
A center of gravity, I attract curiosity
Who thinks my light is a fallacy?

Splitting Attraction

The concept of imagining different forms of attraction in relation to one another has historical precedent. Francis Hutcheson discussed this in his 1728 philosophical text *An Essay on the Nature and Conduct of the Passions and Affections*, through his development of *classes of passions*. These included "how our Passions arise from the Moral Sense, and Sense of Honour" and "how our Passions tend toward the State of others, abstractly from any Consideration of their Moral Qualities," among others. Hutcheson did not mention the word *attraction*, yet spoke in terms that echoed this concept, in one section writing: "Our Affections toward the *Person* arise jointly with our Passions about this Event, according as he acquits himself virtuously or basely."[16] Hutcheson argued that we desire for those who are virtuous to experience happiness and triumph over evil, adding:

> Thus strong Sentiments of *Gratitude*, and vigorous Returns of good Offices observed, raise in the Spectator the highest *Love* and *Esteem* toward both the *Benefactor*, and even the *Person obliged*, with *Security* and *Delight* in virtue.[17]

In essence, Hutcheson wrote of moral virtue as an *attracting* force that should orient our affections toward those who are virtuous if we are good. He warned against a "Pursuit of the Pleasures of the *external senses*, or *Sensuality*" and "the *Voluptuousness* of the external Senses, which by itself would engross the whole Application of our Minds, thro' vain Associations of Ideas."[18] Rather than merely recognizing how different forms of passion may function in relation to one another, Hutcheson

outlined a hierarchical imagining that regarded virtue and sensuality to be opposite forces, predicated on a narrative of good
versus evil; selfless versus selfish; pure versus corrupted.

Almost a century later in 1808, Charles Fourier outlined a
different model via his theory of *passional attraction*. He referred
to various forms of attraction as a guiding force for humanity
that would result in global unity. He argued that this was initiated through the divine, since he interpreted that "God had
given so much influence to passionate attraction and so little to
its enemy, reason." For him, this was designed "to lead us to
the order of the progressive Series [toward actualizing global
unity] in which all aspects of attraction would be satisfied."[19]

Fourier developed an *"analytic and synthetic calculus of passionate attraction* and *repulsion"* to discover a new science of
decoding nature's laws and penetrating its veil of mystery.[20]
The passions in this model were organized into three classes.
The first class related to the five senses, or *"Sensitive Passions,"*
and was described as our attractions to various touches, tastes,
smells, sounds, and sights as motivating forces for our behavior. The second class related to social or affective passions,
which were listed as *Friendship*, *Ambition*, *Love*, and *Paternity or
Family Affection*, and were described as existing "to establish
order and harmony in the social world." The third class related
to the distributive or mechanizing attractions that orient
humanity toward actualizing collective harmony. On the
second class of passional attraction, friendship was defined as
both "love for the whole human race" on a collective level and
"individual attachment without regard for sex" on a personal
level, while ambition was conceived as a force that propels
man forward, and family affection the implanted force that
provokes familial care.[21]

In 1856, Albert Brisbane wrote of a *Theory of the Functions of the Human Passions*, in which he expanded on Fourier's work.[22] Brisbane defined *passional attraction* as "the power that governs the Moral or Spiritual World." He outlined different forms of 'special Attractions,' including those pertaining to the senses: *saporous attraction* to tastes, *odoriferous attraction* to smells, and *sonorous attraction* to sounds. He also described attractions that pertained to other human beings: *benevolent attraction* for friendship and *amatory attraction* for sexual love.[23] Again, these forms of attraction were credited to a "Divine Wisdom." Brisbane clarified that his idea of divinity originated when the Earth, or "the Planet associated with Humanity," implanted attractions in us toward the fulfillment of universal harmony: to "form a harmonious note in the great Concert of the Universe."[24] He believed that "preliminary and incoherent Societies which have existed on the Earth up to the present time" failed to actualize global harmony because they failed to obey attraction.[25] Brisbane included modern industrial capitalist society here:

> Were the false systems of Society that now exist upon the Earth the permanent Destiny of the Human Race, Nature would have given men Attractions adapted to them; she would have given them Attractions for poverty and anxiety, for disorder and antagonism, and the other results which they engender. But as she has not given to men such Attractions, it is a positive demonstration that these Societies are not the permanent Destiny of the Race; that they are to pass away and give place to a Social Order, in which Attraction will find its natural employment and its full satisfaction.[26]

Fourier's and Brisbane's framing of attraction then was not on analyzing how different forms of attraction may function in relation to one another, but on how the functionality of these forms of attraction are interconnected with humanity's inevitable trajectory toward overcoming global disharmony. I have included their framing here because I believe it can inspire us to think about attraction differently. We may consider how splitting attraction can inspire us toward creating interconnected futures in the s p a c e s that such an act creates.

The act of splitting attraction can expand how we think about attraction, thereby affecting our engagement with love, relationship formation, intimacy, and connection. Splitting attraction imagines that there are different forms of attraction that can be *identified* separately or split from one another yet also function simultaneously. The forms of attraction may include but are not limited to (and are not subject to this ordering): sexual, romantic, platonic, sensual, aesthetic, emotional, and intellectual.[27]

Splitting attraction is a conceptual act with material implications, since it can inspire us to envision possibilities and actualize them in our lives. It may guide us to recognize that we can love or be intimate without the presence of sex or romance; that our relational needs are multifaceted beyond cisheteropatriarchy; that we don't have to privilege dominant ideas of what it means to be 'in love;' and that we can nurture all of our relationships outside of hierarchy. To provide more insight into what this can mean, here are a few examples:

Person A is a man who experiences heterosexual attraction. While he is sexually attracted to women, he also desires homosensual bonds with other men. However, since sexuality and gender are heavily policed in conformance with cisheteropatriarchal expectations, he rarely has opportunities to express his sensual attraction toward men without fear of being referred to as 'gay,' which is negatively viewed by his family and peers as being in opposition to a 'real' man.[28]

When attempting to be sensually close with men, he is sometimes rejected and his heterosexuality is questioned. This social policing has alienated and confused him, making him question where he fits in categories of 'straight,' 'gay,' and 'bisexual,' or if he does at all. Rather than continue to express his desire for homosensual bonding, he adheres to a strictly 'hetero' or 'straight' masculine performance, repressing his homosensual feelings internally. As such, his desires that deviate from heteronormativity remain silenced and therefore are assumed by others not to exist. Because of the interconnected nature of attraction with other aspects of self, this creates issues that radiate outward in his life.

Person B is an asexual, aromantic, and agender person who experiences panaesthetic attraction [aesthetic attraction to a person regardless of gender identity]. They experience arousal to others based on their aesthetic appearance and enjoy fantasizing and masturbating to the appearances of others, especially within the context of their kink, but do not themselves desire to engage in sexual or romantic acts with them. Not always certain if this constitutes sexual or romantic attraction, they sometimes find themselves confused if they 'fit' within the definitions of *asexual* and *aromantic*. They are unsure if they are interested in forming a relationship because they have never been shown by potential partners that they are 'worth' the time or energy due to those people's focus on sexual and romantic attraction. Although they are not unhappy being alone, the dominant social expectations that inspire the pursuit of sexual and romantic couplings has left them feeling isolated from others by early adulthood. They are unsure if this is a major issue for them, though, and choose to focus on other things in life for the time being, satisfying their attractions through occasional masturbation.

Person C is a sex-repulsed asexual woman who experiences homoromantic attraction and is interested in finding a lifelong romantic partner. While she enjoys fantasizing about the sexual encounters of other women, she has never had any desire to engage in sex with other women herself. Outside of ace and aro communities, her asexuality is sometimes perceived as invalidating her lesbian identity, with some people assuming that she will 'grow out of' her asexuality rather than accepting that her lesbian-ness can be based in non-sexual attraction. However, she has found that many people within the lesbian community are open to the idea that attraction is not limited by sex. While she has encountered people who look down on her with confusion or pity, her support systems in the lesbian community have helped her learn to become comfortable in her own identity. She continues to find excitement in her search for a lesbian asexual partner, but does not base her fulfillment in life on this relationship formation.

Person D is a bi-oriented demisexual. They do not experience the notion of 'love at first sight' and have only ever developed sexual attraction to people they have been in a deep relationship or friendship with for a long time. From a young age, they recognized that how they experienced attraction failed to meet the expectations of their peers and family members. They found that the term *demisexual* helped them better understand how they experienced attraction and, through that process, have learned to ignore negative criticism from people who reject the notion of demisexuality as 'unnecessary' or simply a preference, as well as to understand that their identity does not necessarily define who they are. They have happily found a partner who understands and affirms how they experience attraction.

If attraction were understood as split rather than hierarchical, we could have more space to prioritize our wellbeing over cisheteropatriarchal pursuits. Splitting attraction can open space for everyone to destabilize the cisheteropatriarchal hierarchy that obscures or devalues various forms of attraction, intimacy, and relationality. However, such an ideological reconfiguration is mired with the challenge of resisting and deconstructing deeply ingrained attitudes regarding how attraction 'naturally' functions between humans. The following sections reflect on different forms of attraction through the approach of analyzing and disentangling them from these dominant assumptions.

Sexual Attraction

Sexual attraction is a term that describes attraction to another person based on the capacity or desire to engage in sexual activity with them. The notion that sexual attraction is inherent to everyone was institutionalized in the nineteenth century through the foundational pillars of sexological discourse. This included the beliefs that all "humans are born with a sexual nature," that sexuality is "at the core of what it means to be human," that sex is "a powerful and driving force in our behavior," and that "the sexual instinct is, by nature, heterosexual."[29] Meanings attached to sexual attraction often equate it to simply being *attraction* itself – that is to say, that attraction *implies* sex. This has generally resulted in other forms of attraction being understood as nothing more than a 'precursor' to sex or as comparatively unimportant.

As will be examined in more detail in Chapters 4 and 5, the heterosexual monogamous romantic coupling has long been upheld in the modern colonial world as the acceptable outlet in which sexual attraction *should* occur. However, not everyone is subject to this demand equally, demonstrated for instance by the way men's disconformity from such a relational formation is often treated far less negatively in comparison to women's. Asexuality, or the lack of sexual attraction, continues to be looked at skeptically or otherwise interpreted as unconditionally impossible. This has led to asexual relationships, whether platonic, romantic, or otherwise, being viewed with ridicule and skepticism.

Historically, the *Boston marriage* or *Wellesley marriage* was an example of a homosocial relationship between unmarried women who were "usually feminists, New Women, [or] often pioneers in a profession."[30] This was a socially accepted relationship in areas of the United States between 1870 and 1920, understood as "neither unnatural nor immoral."[31] These relationships fell out of favor, however, with the rise of sexology discourse, which injected them with sexual meaning and stoked social fears of deviancy. This was aptly summarized by Michelle Gibson:

> To be sure, the sexologists − all male, all interested in the grand taxonomic project of sorting out every type of human behavior and personality − had an agenda to promote: restraint of freedom-seeking women. Their invention of categories of sexual inversion pathologized lesbianism, and ultimately had the effect of ending the benign 'Wellesley marriage' era. After roughly 1920, two women making a home together were at least suspected of deviant behavior, and perhaps also assumed to embody the newly named identity 'lesbian'.[32]

In 1923, British psychologist William Brown commented that "the word 'sexual' is used in its widest sense" to refer to "all feeling of attraction, of affection."[33] By the early 1920s, the idea of *sexual orientation* had become mainstream in the modern colonial world, imbuing sexual meanings into endless expressions of attraction, intimacy, and relationality that may have previously been socially acceptable. As a result, various expressions became interpreted as abnormal or deviant and thus subjected to scrutiny and policing in accordance with the rising social understandings of cisheteropatriarchy upheld by colonial institutions.

New categories of *heterosexual* and *homosexual* effectively merged one's sexual attractions with the Western gender binary. In regard to men being labeled homosexual, this definition came to include men who had "heterosexual desire" yet experienced homosexual attraction "incidental to confinement or to character disturbance," as well as men who were classified as "low in sexual drive" and who had "low male and female hormone content."[34] Men's bodies and social behaviors therefore became subject to intense policing by the twentieth century, since any deviation from the strict heterosexual definition was interpreted as proof of homosexuality. The strict heterosexual definition was also applied to women. In the early twentieth century, sexologists openly advocated for women and girls to be subject to intense social policing, warning that "many of the acts which we look upon as perfectly normal and natural should, in reality, be classed scientifically as perversions."[35] Any wavering from 'strictly heterosexual' performance became scrutinized through the social policing of everyday behaviors under the ever-present threats of ostracization, pathologization, and criminalization.

Splitting attraction could reorient social norms to re-accept relationships and expressions that were not always viewed as abnormal or unnatural. While sexological discourses have undeniably cast a long shadow over how we understand attraction today, we can destabilize its foundations through our collective refusal. Rather than pursuing inclusion within it via another neatly defined label, we can not only shift the lines of what constitutes 'natural' and 'unnatural' in the Western worldview, but erase them altogether by exposing the foundations on which those lines were drawn. This would of course include deconstructing the belief that attraction is inherently sexual or, as Arthur Tansley wrote in 1920, that the "tender instinct" cannot be split from the sexual one.[36]

Romantic Attraction

Romantic attraction is a term that describes attraction to another person based on the capacity or desire to engage in romantic acts or form a romantic relationship with them. As will be discussed in more depth in Chapter 5, the concept of romantic love took prominence through the Romantic movement in Europe and was used to uphold colonial supremacy in love hierarchies that positioned the non-European as incapable of romantic or 'true' love.

Scores of colonial missions throughout the world operated as sites of religious conversion in the nineteenth century, preaching the gospel of Protestant evangelicalism that framed salvation on individual terms. Missions not only preached what Europeans saw as the religious gospel, but shifted social values of the colonized toward individualism, which in turn placed "a greater emphasis on the ethics, and the mechanics, of romantic attraction," as noted by Claire McLisky. To fulfill this expectation not only required finding the ideal partner in accordance with European cisheteropatriarchal constructs, but also religious constructs: to "cherish loved ones without allowing the special affections felt for them to diminish the love felt for Christ."[37] Through colonialism, romantic attraction became normalized as the expression of 'true love' between couples and the basis of the sanctified familial institution.

Aromanticism, or the lack of romantic attraction, is more misunderstood and made invisible than asexuality because of how it expands notions of attraction beyond the sexual in its mere definition. Even as it describes its absence, aromanticism asks for the recognition of *romantic attraction* as a form of attraction that is not inherently entangled with sexual attraction. Furthermore, because "society tends to value romantic above non-romantic relationships and considers sexual behaviors as a fundamental aspect of those relationships," aros may internalize that they are destined for lifelong unfulfillment.[38] Embracing and affirming aromanticism can be part of the movement toward reorienting social norms and destabilizing the idea that the pursuit of relationships predicated on romantic attraction is a necessary part of living a fulfilled life.

Platonic Attraction

Platonic attraction is a term that describes attraction to another person based on the capacity or desire to form a close bond or friendship with them. As will be further explained in Chapter 5, the concept of platonic love originated from Marsilio Ficino's fifteenth-century interpretations of affection between males, one older and one younger, in Ancient Greece.[39] This was the "mystical love of men for one another, the union of two human souls in a single perfect friendship," as described by classics scholar Benjamin Jowett.[40]

Definitions of platonic love changed in the following centuries to describe attraction between men and women, such as
in an 1868 discussion of the concept by William Rounseville
Alger, who defined it as "a wholly free and elective friendship" and "a high personal passion [. . .] with the exception
that no physical influence of sex enters into it."[41] Platonic
friendships between men and women were more often than
not viewed with skepticism, if not regarded as outright preposterous, with the common belief that "the sexes can't cross
except in [romantic] love."[42]

This was entangled with ideas of maturity. For men, it was
believed that a mature man could simply not love a woman
platonically.[43] A woman was deemed to be only capable of
forming platonic relationships with a man if "she intends the
man to make love to her after she has had enough of the preliminary nonsense, or [if] she is a flirt and has no intention of
taking him seriously," as written by Gertrude Atherton for
The Lady's Realm magazine.[44] Platonic attraction between
men and women was thus often viewed as unconditionally
impossible – an idea that persists today.

However, some commentators in the late nineteenth and
early twentieth centuries noted that such platonic relationships or friendships between men and women were in fact
possible, even if difficult to achieve. In 1884, Benjamin
Jowett wrote that such friendships "are very likely to become
foolish" and advised that "only by great care is it possible to
avoid this."[45] C. Heyland Fox professed at the turn of the
century that it was only the behavior of women that could
"keep such friendship on the plane of platonism," concluding that "if she is too weak to do so, or does not wish to, then
she will generally find the man willing and ready to cross the
line."[46]

In 1919, E. R. Nash provided examples of platonic relationships he knew personally, including a couple who lived together in close intimacy 'as brother and sister.' Nash explained that the man gratified his sexual desires with another woman "for who he only has physical affection," noting that his wife "does not object to her lover's sexual association with other women." Nash also wrote that the woman the man was involved with sexually was married and "adores her husband, but for her sexual gratification she prefers her paramour." It was only under situations of what Nash described as "sexual stress" that the two met up.[47] In 1921, Arthur Belleville McCoid noted a similar case of a man and woman who married on the basis of "sensible and platonic attraction." He wrote that the couple had developed "a deep mutual understanding and do not interfere with each other's personal habits and freedom."[48]

These cases might be understood as reflecting a form of poly-relationality, where the satisfaction of potential sexual needs is found outside of marriage while platonic satisfaction is found in marriage. These cases exemplify historical depth to such formations. They can also provoke us to consider how understanding attraction as multilayered or split today can result in the formation of various relationships, such as where one partner is not expected to service all of every person's relational needs within a cisheteropatriarchal nuclear family dynamic.

As another historical dimension, historians have noted that platonic friendships between men, which may be referred to as homosocial, were common among men in Europe prior to the rise of Christianity. "The history of male friendship in the West is a story of a long decline, from overt sexual relationships through to a highly codified set of permissible interactions where sexuality was to be the element least sought," write

Richard Cleminson and Francisco V. García. Homosociality among men became clouded in skepticism by the nineteenth century, "surrounded by prohibition and distance in order to avoid any carnal contact," where social fears around homosociality were institutionalized through pathologizing 'scientific' discourses.[49] However, platonic friendships among men remained common, even as they were increasingly policed by social expectations regarding what was and was not 'appropriate' for a man, particularly with consideration to avoiding being labeled homosexual. By the twentieth century, heterosexual men's "desire to establish (apparently) nonsexual friendship and brotherhood" was an important part of situating themselves as 'real men' in a male-dominated society.[50] Homosocial bonds between heterosexual men were maintained through the "use of women as changeable, perhaps symbolic, property"[51] along with homophobic comradeship.[52]

Platonic friendships among women are generally not based in such performative displays of heterosexual desire, objectification, or overt homophobia. They are also generally not socially scrutinized to the same degree as men's relationships. This is largely because women's relationships are treated as 'unimportant' in comparison to men's relationships under cisheteropatriarchy. Historians have long noticed the absence of record regarding women's friendships.[53] Women's relationships were so obscured that a commentator asserted in 1914 that "friendship is almost an entirely masculine emotion."[54] However, platonic friendships were recognized by others as having a relatively high popularity between women at the start of the twentieth century, which was attributed to women's 'natural' gravitation toward tenderness.[55]

In the early 2000s, Barbara J. Bank wrote that relationships between women were assumed to be homosocial, or otherwise platonic, by default, referring to the differences surrounding assumptions about the words *boyfriend* and *girlfriend*. When a woman talks about a boyfriend, the relationship is assumed to be romantic and sexual, yet when she talks about a girlfriend she means "a homosocial relationship lacking in sexual and romantic potential." Bank explained that the dominance of these social assumptions marginalizes and excludes the possibility of *heterosocial* relationships between women and men as well as homosexual relationships between women. This has effectively created prevailing social conditions in which heterosocial relationships are always seen as inherently imbued with assumptions of romance and sex while, at the same time, "much social effort goes into maintaining the line between homosocial and homosexual relationships and into denying the sexual and romantic potential of same-sex friendships."[56]

The dominant perception that platonic attraction between men and women is both absurd in practice and dangerous to romantic relationships has undoubtedly stifled the formation of intimate friendships between men and women. This is not without consequence or loss.[57] C. Heyland Fox expressed that platonic love can be "as strong, as tender, and as faithful as any love between two people in more intimate relation to each other."[58] Yet, platonic friendships are often treated as disposable in comparison to romantic relationships, which can, as Sherronda Brown noted in 2022, create grief that comes from "being repeatedly abandoned, disregarded, and disposed of by others to make way for their romantic ventures." By prioritizing friendships and community bonds "as precious gifts to be treasured, as prosperous gardens to be nurtured," this hierarchy of relationships may be effectively undermined.[59] A world in which platonic bonds are valued just as much, if not more, than romantic ones might also be more oriented toward community and cooperation rather than individualism and competition.

Sensual Attraction

Sensual attraction is a term that describes attraction to another person based on the capacity or desire to be sensually close with them. In its broader definition, sensual attraction does not necessarily have to involve physical touch, since it relates to all of the senses, although it is most often discussed in the context of touch. Sensual attraction is almost exclusively conceived of as an essential part of, or a representation of, romantic and sexual attraction. This is the social belief that sexual passion "only endures so long as the power of sensual attraction possessed by its object" does not falter.[60]

Sensual attraction or intimacy has been characterized historically as dangerous and disruptive for centuries – a reflection of a lower or more 'animalistic' form of bodily desire in comparison to the morally superior form of virtuous love expressed through the institution of marriage. As proclaimed by Oliver Phelps Brown in 1874, unrestrained sensual attraction was a quality inherent to "those of the lowest grades of society or savage races, where chastity is unknown as a virtue."[61] To achieve 'restraint' over one's sensual attraction was interpreted as a marker of being 'civilized.' As an underlying sexual attraction became increasingly presumed to be ever-present, sensual closeness became highly policed along codified lines in the modern colonial world, only acceptable in certain controlled contexts.

Sensual attraction was the subject of much controversy in the nineteenth century. Christian ministers such as Adin

Ballou wrote that sensual amativeness, or the arousal of sensual feelings, was a quality of beasts that existed in opposition to "spiritual and moral intelligence."[62] Magazine articles in the period promoted similar sentiments among the public.[63] In opposition stood the free love movement, which critiqued this hierarchization of attraction. Free love writer Austin Kent, for instance, wrote in 1857 that "this whole argument of two radical and diverse manifestations of amativeness in man, is unphilosophical and absurd." Kent further professed that "it is not true that any man ever ultimates love entirely disconnected with its spiritual element," refusing the idea that men of so called 'lower races' were strictly sensual.[64]

Although sensual attraction was most commonly discussed as reflecting sexual attraction between men and women, this was also assumed to be true for members of the same gender, couched in the usual homophobic hysteria. Homosensual closeness between women was feared by Western scientists in the early twentieth century as a potential cause and signifier of homosexuality. In 1922, Paul Bousfield expressed concern over "women who delight to hold hands, to kiss one another rather passionately, to visit one another's bedrooms and inspect clothing," writing that this was evidence of homosexuality. Bousfield made this claim on the basis that "if men were to perform some of the acts which we have described, everyone would suspect them of being homosexual."[65] Arthur Tansley similarly warned that "It may be objected that physical caresses between members of the same sex are more naturally considered as expressions of the tender instinct than of the sexual instinct. But this is certainly not the case." Tansley reinforced the idea that physical touch is imbued with sexual meaning and commented: "this country at least [England], completely bars any physical expression [among men] of the sort that is so common among women," and identified this as a positive attribute.[66] Johannes Hermanus van der Hoop further advised for children to be closely watched, claiming that "physical touch may easily arouse sexual emotions, which may then be directed towards the same sex."[67]

These reports demonstrate how homophobic fears over sensual bonding between men were well established as part of Western medical practice by the early twentieth century, while further calls to impose social policing on women and children were also present. Given the timeline of these reports, it is clear that sensual attraction or bonding between members of the same gender was not always imbued with sexual meanings. Yet, attempting to delink sensual attraction from its sexual and romantic assumptions still remains an issue today.

This was recently reflected through the case of Cuddlr, an app that launched in 2014 with the objective to coordinate exclusively sensual meetups. Charlie Williams, the developer of the app, expressed an awareness of the way sensual touch was dominantly perceived:

> Cuddling takes communication, respect for boundaries, and self-control. Some people will, of course, want to do more than cuddle. [. . .] Sex is a great thing too, but there are other apps for that. Use those ones if that's what you're looking for. Use Cuddlr when you want to hold and be held, to feel like all is right with the world, and to have a simple connection without expectation.[68]

Many media outlets responded with skepticism at the app's objective, asserting that it was completely unrealistic and unattainable. An article for Salon ran with the sarcastic subheading: 'In a totally nonsexual way, they swear!' The author wrote that the app was based on a "platonic ideal" that was not realistic in practice.[69] A writer for the *Washington Post* wrote that Cuddlr challenged cultural norms by attempting to delink sensual attraction from its sexual and romantic associations. However, they also problematized anyone who would use such an application: "only the socially destitute would rely on such an app."[70] Interestingly, the author also indicated: "I hugged one of my co-workers this morning after spotting him on Cuddlr. It was nice!"[71]

Comparative cultural consideration provides a different angle as to why an app such as Cuddlr may have been created in the first place and attained over 200,000 downloads in its first week alone.[72] An article for Tech Times by Lauren Keating briefly spoke to the way physical touch between strangers, especially men, was scrutinized more in Western cultures than elsewhere.[73] Charlie Williams himself explained that part of his intention behind developing the app was to challenge dominant assumptions surrounding sensual closeness between heterosexual men:

> Growing up, I've experienced the gradual dropping away of physical affection from same-sex friends as homophobia and awkwardness sets in, and as that same energy is refocused toward dating and relationships. [. . .] We need to delve deeper, to go beyond rejecting cliché and start actually challenging the ways we interact (or the ways we don't feel we are allowed to interact).[74]

Finding ways to reintegrate sensual closeness in our lives, if it is absent or infrequent, has also been interconnected with potentially improving health and wellbeing. Diana Raab for *Psychology Today* writes: "If you're able to engage in sensual behaviors on a regular basis, it can permeate many aspects of your life by making you feel more alive and playful, and less stressed and depressed." For this reason, Raab advocates for the disentangling of sensuality from its sexual connotations: "Sensuality is an important part of intimacy and sexuality, but as mentioned above, it's not necessarily connected."[75]

Despite a high-profile release, Cuddlr was plagued by logistical challenges from being understaffed, and closed in early 2015.[76] It briefly relaunched as Spoonr the same year, yet closed again in early 2017. In a 2018 article for *Paper Mag*, Beatrice Hazlehurst speculated that Spoonr was misused by "people with motives that contradicted the app's mission statement." Hazlehurst believed that the app's objective to disentangle sensual and sexual intimacy was important and especially relevant to "lonely millennials, [who] aren't touching each other platonically," summarizing that "there are very few places to turn if you want to be held, rather than fucked." However, Hazlehurst concluded that "we shouldn't need more technology to rectify that."[77] A cultural shift to normalize sensual intimacy without sexual or romantic connotations might achieve this result, yet it remains a slow walk toward deconstructing how we think about sensuality.

For aros and aces who do experience sensual attraction, being attracted to someone sensually but not sexually or romantically can be alienating. Others may cast people in search of sensual but not sexual pleasure as 'abnormal,' 'creepy,' or 'socially destitute,' and it remains difficult for some people to imagine how a person could really "just want to cuddle."[78]

However, people in certain subcultures, such as the kink and BDSM subculture, may be more accepting of such a possibility. This is because desiring sensual intimacy without sexual or romantic expectations may simply be seen as an acceptable aspect of one's kink, rather than a problem with one's personhood. Despite the mainstream assumption that kink is inherently sexual, people within the subculture often have a different view. Scholar Lorca Jolene Sloan suggests that because participants set the boundaries for a play session before engagement and form relationships built on trust in the process, sex does not have to be an expectation.[79] The boundaries of a session can be both physical and psychological, in which participants can even establish that 'scenes will not cause them to feel sexual desire' and that 'partners should not expect or hope for the scene to have this effect.' For this reason, Sloan concludes that kink and BDSM may be generative spaces for aces because they can 'form partnerships based on attractions they *do* feel and fantasies they *do* wish to realize.'[80] This was reverberated by kinky ace writer Bob O'Boyle, who noted in an article for *AZE* that "It's not sex that I crave, it's physical affection."[81]

Aesthetic Attraction

Aesthetic attraction is a term that describes attraction to another person based on their visual appearance. Aesthetic attraction can be interpreted as a form of sensual attraction, since it involves the sense of sight, but is usually discussed independently. A person who experiences aesthetic attraction toward another person desires to see them frequently and derives pleasure from the experience. One of the most common framings of aesthetic attraction is that it is comparable to appreciating a beautiful piece of art or natural landscape. This is how it was framed on AVEN's former 'Questions Asked by Asexual and Questioning People' page in 2003 (one of the earliest references to aesthetic attraction): "Many asexuals can see that other people are aesthetically attractive to them but see this beauty as no different from looking at a beautiful painting or a stunning sunset."[82] While some people who expressed their views in online discussions resonate with this metaphor, others prefer to make a distinction between what they see as 'attraction' versus 'appreciation,' while still others argue that such a distinction should not exist, indicating that aesthetic attraction can be interpreted in various respects.

Similar to platonic and sensual attraction, there is a general assumption that a person automatically has sexual and romantic attraction toward a person whom they are aesthetically attracted to. In an article for *Archer*, Nicole Brinkley conveys this through an example: "I think Jason Momoa is one of the most attractive people on the planet. I don't want to have sex with Jason Momoa. This used to confuse my friends."[83] Identifying this distinction can sometimes be difficult, even for aces and aros who are familiar with different forms of attraction. In online discussions, some aces and aros have expressed challenges with identifying whether their aesthetic feelings emerged from aesthetic attraction or sexual/romantic attraction. Some noted how the enjoyment they received from looking at certain people through statements such as 'I enjoyed looking at people' or 'I like people-watching' led them to believe they were not ace or aro, thinking this to be a signification of a romantic crush or of sexual feelings.

While I personally do not experience sexual or romantic attraction, I am attracted to the visual appearance *usually* of people who are men (which is the basis for my gravitation toward the label gay), knowing that the Western gender binary has erected borders in our brains and trained our eyes to categorize gender based on various visual markers. While it may seem like an unnecessary technicality, those of us who experience aesthetic attraction are often not 'exclusively' attracted to any gender, since we are attracted to a person's visual appearance, not their gender identity. Other aces and aros in online discussions have similarly identified the experience with their aesthetic attraction transcending the borders of gender identity. Some users have spoken of being 'generally' attracted to people whose appearances fit within stereotypical ideas of a 'masculine man' or 'feminine woman,' even if that person did not identify by that gender.

More generally this exposes how aesthetic attraction can be both gendered and ungendered simultaneously. The orienting notions of 'femininity' and 'masculinity' have come to dominantly shape whose appearances are deemed attractive and therefore influences how our appearances are aesthetically interpreted. A recent study of dominant attitudes concerning gendered appearances noted: "Highly feminine or highly masculine human qualities are considered highly attractive," even being associated with more healthy relationships and attractive offspring.[84]

The colonial (il)logics and hierarchies of 'race' and 'ethnicity' have similarly shaped who is deemed aesthetically attractive, with whiteness upheld as exemplary of beauty and attractiveness. While upon colonial contact whiteness was not necessarily idolized, over many years of conditioning, colonialism shifted attitudes of beauty. There is an extensive historical record demonstrating how 'Europeanness' was presented as the pinnacle of beauty throughout the burgeoning modern colonial world.

In 1822, US politician George Tucker argued: "Even an African taste would commonly think an European beauty handsomer than one of his own tribe," further claiming that this was also true of "the Indians," who reportedly "had no hesitation in saying that they thought our women much handsomer than their own."[85] In 1844, German travel writer Johann Georg Kohl expressed that the most beautiful African woman "must still be far inferior in loveliness to a European beauty."[86] Knight Dunlap, former president of the American Psychological Association, wrote in 1920 that "The type which is highest in value tends to approximate the European type, whenever the European type becomes known," asserting that "All dark races prefer white skin, and it is a general rule that the female of the inferior race prefers the male of the superior race to the male of her own race" as well as that "the inferior male considers the superior female more beautiful than the female of his own race."[87] This 'scientific' claim on beauty was entwined with eugenics and ideas of ensuring "racial betterment."[88] The legacies of this discourse remain prevalent today, becoming internalized and reproduced through generations. The widely recognized 'doll study' in the 1940s demonstrated its reach in Black children between the ages of three and seven in the United States, where whiteness was associated by the children with positive characteristics and Blackness with negative attributes.[89] This study was also executed in the Caribbean in 1995 and demonstrated a similar result, with the author attributing this negative self-image to colonialism.[90]

The now normalized pursuit of 'white beauty' is also connected to familial formation. Adolfo Gamboa reflected on this issue in Latin American contexts in an article for *AZE*:

Since we were kids, we have been told that we should be like 'beautiful people' – white, athletic, rich, able-bodied – and that the pinnacle of love was sex. We grew up hearing that we had to admire and aspire to be with these alluring people, so that we could have sex with them and have nice children: 'hay que mejorar la raza.'[91]

This common phrase to 'improve the race' has been described as "an allusion to the desirability of relationships with people who are whiter than oneself."[92]

While these narratives can be rejected, they are powerful orienting forces that often go unquestioned. Contemporary discourses on beauty have continued to reflect this through ideas of 'racial preference,' which was found in a 2021 study to be "systematically motivated by negative attitudes toward particular races."[93] Despite another study indicating that a person who openly reveals that they have 'racial preferences' is more likely to be perceived as "more racist, less attractive, [and] less dateable,"[94] this has not necessarily altered people actually having preferences, and has possibly buried discussions about them. Because colonialism continues to influence how we experience attraction, we cannot simply ignore its presence, but rather are tasked with considering how it is implicated in our attractions.

This is not only limited to 'race' or 'ethnicity,' but is also entwined with body size. This was demonstrated through the colonial narrative that non-Europeans were historically attracted to fatness: "Nineteenth-century European and American writers didn't just describe African and Asian people as fat but insisted that they revered fatness."[95] Contemporary historian Christopher E. Forth noted that around the late eighteenth century "a growing number of authors observed that certain non-Western peoples profoundly admired corpulence and would, if they had the means, seek to make themselves as large as possible."[96] This was framed as 'proof' of, again, white supremacy and the allegedly 'uncivilized' and 'primitive nature' of 'lower races.'

Henry T. Finck, an influential critic of the period, wrote in *Primitive Love and Love-Stories* (1899) that "among the uncivilized and Oriental races in general, fat is the criterion of feminine attractiveness" and that this attraction was even the case among "coarse men (*i.e.*, most men)" in Europe and America as well.[97] Finck and other social critics implied that it was only among 'civilized' or 'refined' men that fatness was unattractive. Contemporary scholar Sabrina Strings identified that this narrative was also present in popular literature of the period, such as in an 1897 article from *Harper's Bazaar* by Edith Bigelow entitled 'The Sorrows of the Fat.' In the article, Bigelow wrote: "The stout lady of five-and-thirty has to remain stout. It is her nature – hereditary, possibly – and all she can hope for is not to become *obese*. That is the state all persons of refinement must shun."[98] *Anti-fatness* functioned as a signifier of civilization; a narrative guarded by Western cultural authorities, who popularized "the association of heaviness with unacceptable savagery that continues today."[99]

This demonstrates how aesthetic attraction actively intersects with larger social currents in the modern colonial world. For instance, Da'Shaun L. Harrison writes: "Beauty standards, especially in the United States, are predicated on anti-Blackness, anti-fatness, anti-disfiguredness, cisheterosexism, and ableism."[100] As will be discussed in Chapter 5, the capacity for aesthetic judgment itself was upheld through the colonial project as only being possible by the European subject.[101] It is perhaps of no surprise then that anti-poor, anti-Black, anti-fat, anti-disfigured, cisheterosexist, and ableist (il)logics have come to dominantly shape who is considered aesthetically attractive and who is not. It is equally unsurprising that aesthetic pursuits are often undertaken to conform to the image and lifestyle of what the European subject has preached and upheld as beautiful and to destroy or denigrate what it has marked as repulsive. This has influenced how we engage in consumption habits to appear 'beautiful,' how we orient our lives in pursuit of 'success' and 'wealth,' how we relate to nature, and elsewise, what we pursue in life.

Emotional Attraction

Emotional attraction is a term that describes attraction to someone's personality, their social and self-awareness, or their emotional relationality. In a 2019 Healthline article, Cindy Lamonthe wrote that emotional attraction can be "developed based on things like the other person's values, their personality, and how they show they care." Signifiers of one's emotional attraction may be feeling like you are "seen or heard from the other person" or that they are nurturing to you.[102] People who could be assumed by others to be romantically and sexually interested in one another may feel obstructed from forming emotional connections with others – such as by engaging in intimate conversations – because of romantic and sexual assumptions.

Aros and aces may know this feeling all too well when we reach out and make connections with others that are misread as expressions of romantic and sexual attraction. At the same time, forming an emotional bond with someone may also inspire feelings of romantic and sexual attraction. This is reflected through *demiromanticism* and *demisexuality*, terms to describe the development of romantic and sexual attraction, respectively, for a person after an emotional bond is established.[103]

Emotional attraction or love was another concept used in the 'love hierarchies' of 'civilization.' In 1915, eugenicist Selwyn Gould Langley defined love as a "mental-emotional-attraction," asserting that "love came later when the mental qualities, and emotions, became highly developed in the human body." This definition of love he placed in opposition to "idealized-physical-attraction," subsequently asking how a "normal race" of people could be produced through mental-emotional-attraction.[104]

However, even as it was deemed part of the 'superior' love, emotional attraction alone was often not considered sufficient for relationship formation. In 1905, Charles Whitby leveraged the critique that "unions consummated under mere emotional attraction" would be insufficient for a lasting marriage without being reinforced by a "moral" or "rational" commitment.[105] Albert Wilson similarly warned in 1910 that "the civil marriage might be described as based on common sense, affection, or some other emotional attraction, and may be entirely devoid of religious sentiment," which made it vulnerable to instability. Wilson advised couples to mutually embrace commitment to religious duty to fortify such emotional bonds.[106]

In the late twentieth century, emotional attraction became associated with the newly created 'science' of *emotional intelligence*, aimed at measuring a person's individual capacity to diagnose and monitor "the internal environment of their own and others' minds" to demonstrate "remarkable skillfulness in managing their relationships with others in ways that produce winning outcomes." Emotional intelligence was gauged via 'objective' metrics on "a scale of emotional attractiveness on which every individual will fall, and the higher the position on the scale, the greater the success of a person in his or her social environment."[107] This 'science' of emotion reinforced the pursuit of 'success' in the modern colonial world, with studies addressing the benefits of emotional intelligence in the capitalist workplace as "intrapersonal skills" and "mood management."[108] Just as *aesthetic attraction* became defined through colonial structures, *emotional attraction* became dominantly valued based on one's ability to control one's emotions within such structures.[109]

At the turn of the twenty-first century, the presence of *hookup culture* in the mass media shaped ideas about so-called casual sex, which was often defined as "hooking up only when drunk, refraining from tenderness, being unfriendly afterward, and avoiding 'repeat' hookups."[110] Hooking up is sometimes portrayed as a reflection of the individual benefits of emotional detachment.[111] For instance, Reilly Kincaid argues that women may find that this emotionless element of hookup culture provides them with "greater control over social impressions" to forge "empowered social images," even as it still aligns with "dominant gender norms legitimating heteronormative scripts that entitle men to pursue women."[112] Emotional attraction can therefore be interpreted as a stumbling block to casual sex, since it can bring unwanted meaning to such encounters.

Much of this chapter has been devoted to addressing the possibilities of what might happen when we split non-sexual attractions from their presumed sexual meanings, reaching the familiar conclusion that it can encourage generative forms of intimacy and connectivity that may have otherwise been obscured or devalued by the overbearing presence of sexuality. Hookup culture asks us to consider 'the inverse' approach – where the sexual has been 'detached' or 'unhooked' from the emotional, rather than vice versa. It reveals how the act of splitting attraction from the 'top down' rather than from the 'bottom up' results in different conclusions; that sex has the social power to relinquish itself from its perceived attachments in a way that other attractions do not.

Intellectual Attraction

Intellectual attraction is a term that describes attraction to a person's psychological, intellectual, or mental expressions. Intellectual attraction has been described as having "more to do with what or how a person thinks instead of the person themselves."[113] While it is often equated to attraction to a person's intelligence,[114] the term may be defined in various respects. In online discussions, some aces and aros have expressed how everyone has their own qualities that they find attractive about how someone else thinks, although they noted that these can also be shaped by the dominant culture. The term *psychological attraction* has been defined based on a person's attraction to people "similar enough to ourselves to make us feel safe," who have "characteristics that challenge and excite us," and who encourage us to confront "unresolved pain."[115]

In the early twentieth century, intellectual attraction was presented with a moralist agenda. In *Woman and Socialism* (1910), German politician August Bebel declared:

> Satisfaction of the sexual impulse is essential to the sound physical and mental development of man and woman. But man has gone beyond the animal stage, and so is not contented by mere physical satisfaction of his sexual impulse. He requires intellectual attraction as well [. . .] Where such intellectual harmony fails to exist, the sexual intercourse is purely mechanical and thereby becomes immoral. Men and women

of refinement demand a mutual attraction that extends beyond their sexual relations.[116]

This framing was commonly appealed to by religious moralists of the period to emphasize how marriages should not be primarily based on sexual attraction, but on intellectual moral harmony. This was echoed in Volume II of *A Handbook of Moral Theology* (1919), where Antony Koch argued that because "sensual and intellectual attraction" naturally attracted the two sexes for the purposes of stimulation, "the gratification of the sexual instinct [was] not a sufficient moral motive to justify marriage."[117]

Intellectual attraction became discussed as essential to a healthy and sustainable relationship. At the end of the twentieth century, Ayala Malach Pines wrote that the absence of mutual intellectual attraction could result in relationship burnout, including when one partner is viewed as 'intelligent' by others, but their partner does not draw meaning from the ways in which they're viewed as intelligent. Pines explained that couples who experienced low relationship burnout cited "intellectual attraction as a very important and stimulating part of their relationship" and thus concluded that "couples who have independent minds and interests are better able to challenge each other and to maintain an intellectual spark in the relationship."[118]

Intellectual attraction came to serve as the basis of the 'controversial' term *sapiosexual*. The identity was created by LiveJournal user wolfieboy, who wrote a brief blog post explaining how they defined the term:

Me? I don't care too much about the plumbing. I want an incisive, inquisitive, insightful, irreverent mind. I want someone

for whom philosophical discussion is foreplay. I want someone who sometimes makes me go ouch due to their wit and
evil sense of humor. [. . .] I decided all that means that I am
sapiosexual. I want to fuck with people's minds.[119]

Sapiosexuality regards one's sexual attraction to be dependent
on one's intellectual attraction, rather than sexual attraction
being the 'primary driver.' Most of the comments to this post
were receptive to the new term and sought to spread awareness of it. There was a humorous tone to wolfieboy's post,
even including a self-admission: "I invented this term while
on too little sleep driving up from SF in the summer of '98
and I'm trying to propagate it as much as possible. So please
use it when appropriate." Yet, sapiosexuality was not simply
framed as a dismissible joke.[120] Following the publication of
this post, many people gravitated toward the term to describe
how they experienced attraction.

Sapiosexual was used sparingly throughout the 2000s,
appearing in a few scattered media articles. However, the
term gained traction in the next few years, especially after
online dating platform OkCupid announced its inclusion
on their services, arguably bringing the term mainstream
visibility.[121] With the increasing coverage, a rising wave of
criticism targeted the concept as ableist, classist, and founded
on a reductionist perspective of intelligence. A 2016 article
for VICE stated that the identity "makes you look like a pretentious asshat."[122] *Sapiosexual* continued to be criticized by
more people and various outlets, eventually causing
OkCupid to remove the term from their platform by 2019
"after considerable negative feedback."[123]

Despite this, *sapiosexual* continued to acquire recognition,
being added to the Merriam-Webster dictionary in 2020.[124]

However, when sapiosexuality was mentioned, it was now often with the caveat that the term had some potentially problematic implications, such as in an article for WebMD:

> Some people believe that sapiosexuality devalues people with different mental abilities. Those who label it as elitist or Eurocentric claim that it over-values Western education and IQ while ignoring other forms of intelligence. Defenders of sapiosexuality claim that it's based on relationship compatibility rather than a judgment of absolute worth.[125]

If a person constructs their intellectual attraction on metrics that privilege IQ or hierarchical notions of intelligence, how they experience attraction may very well be elitist. For example, one self-identified sapiosexual man stated in a 2018 interview: "If I find a person physically or otherwise attractive, but they seem stupid, I lose all attraction. If someone is not so physically or otherwise attractive, but they seem smart, there's a good chance I'm turned on."[126] To critics, statements like these make sapiosexual identity seem pretentious.

The problematic cloud surrounding sapiosexuality has likely obscured and dissuaded some people from identifying intellectual attraction as legitimate. This may provoke us to consider how identities can also individualize how we think about concepts, erecting barriers that divide us into different types of people that must fight for acceptance and inclusion. Even as identities can help provide visibility to concepts – albeit largely a visibility that reinforces the lines of dominant discourses – they can also distract us from our relationality.

The Queerness of Space

This analysis of these various terms for attraction – sexual, romantic, platonic, sensual, aesthetic, emotional, and intellectual – destabilizes the concept of sexual orientation as defining our attractions. It presents some of the many ways attraction may function in our lives and exposes the colonial roots of these concepts which sprouted out of a pursuit to demarcate the 'civilized' and the 'uncivilized'; the 'superior' and the 'inferior'; the 'loveful' and the 'loveless'; the 'beautiful' and the 'repugnant'; the 'attractive' and the 'unattractive.' This review was not undertaken to reproduce a 'science' of attraction nor to claim and defend the ways in which it must exist. Rather, the previous forms of attraction are points of intervention to inspire critical reflection; to see new possibilities, relational formations, expressions, intimacies, connections, and communities. Splitting attraction is an act that reveals to us the queerness of space – the space to understand and express the complexities of our existence rather than reducing ourselves to the either/or constructs of the modern colonial world. How we use this space determines whether the act of splitting attraction becomes an avenue to simply recreate another 'scientific' model of attraction or to crack the foundation of the cisheteropatriarchal order, revealing the artificiality of borders that have been erected in an attempt to divide what may be referred to as *the queer*.

Queerness, in this sense, represents the essence of the universe that is only labeled as 'queer' in itself because the 'god complex' of the 'ordered world' has marked it as 'unnatural' – despite the queer being more in line with the reality of the transformative, fluid, chaotic, and ever-changing nature of the universe we live in. Since human beings are a lifeform inherent to the transformative universe, it would only make sense that queerness is human nature.

The colonizers generally upheld that no territory could go unclaimed and that spaces where non-Europeans lived were *terra nullius* (no *Man's* land) or, in their eyes, open to their desires, in line with the "extensive documentation of how this sort of classic sexualized colonial imagery casts resource-rich newly found lands as like women's bodies in a patriarchal world, available for both loving and dominating/raping."[127] Colonizers learned to fabricate justifications to assert control over space, claiming that Indigenous peoples were 'morally destitute.' This pattern of the colonizer framing themselves as cleanser and defender remains present today as a means of claiming the right to control material and immaterial space: bodies, minds, narratives, and futures.

Although labels occupy metaphysical space, we can see the parallels here with colonialism's attempts to define and control physical space. In 2011, Chrystos spoke to the relationship between the trajectory of word configuration and physical space in a public talk:

> It occurs to me that you may not have heard someone speak in this way. There's no Point A to B. This is Indian Country. It has no fences. It doesn't judge people by their bank accounts, but by how much they do for their community. I would suggest to you that Indian Country has many ideas about how to behave correctly. I ask you to consider Indigenous leadership rather than tokenism.[128]

Chrystos here reminds us of the underlying implications of word configurations on how we see the world. The obvious differences between colonial and Indigenous visions demonstrates how even the way we speak can be mirrored in the environment (i.e. that fences in our environment can reflect fences in our minds and vice versa).

Identity labels are often rooted in the metaphysical space claims of Western 'scientific' experts who pathologized, classified, and studied human behavior through discourses that regulated and controlled colonial populations. So why should we approach the notion of identity labels today, undoubtedly rooted and shaped by such an agenda, as 'neutral' or infallible permutations of human existence? What is the 'end game' of this pursuit to define ourselves by Western claims? Once we have defined every permutation, every splintered detail of ourselves, what then?

Rather than attempt to issue definitive responses to impossible questions, I rest in the queerness of space, not arguing for an immediate dissolution of labels, which would be unrealistic anyway, but for an awareness that to obsessively pursue the confines of 'understanding' in the colonial 'god complex' is a pursuit that stands in opposition to the queerness of space, by which I mean the universe.

And what if the dimensional split
Opened and the world fell out
Of orbit and we reached across the borders
And what if . . .
We did everything we thought we could not
And it became our oblivion
Endless, opening, closing
In the ordered world the spaces reportedly vanished
As if nothing was beyond our reach
And so it seemed like queerness was over

But the 'wild' remains
Even under symbols of false claim
How arrogant it is to assume
Control over the wondrous
And believe in all your self-importance
That you could really kill
The queer

3

The Cyberspatial Emergence
of Asexual Identity

> I am an asexual person wondering if my lack of sexual inter-
> est might doom me to relative loneliness – a life with many
> good and special friends, but without a lifelong, deeply
> loving, committed bond to anyone.[1]

This was a post made in 1990, by a user referred to here as B,
that opened a discussion topic entitled 'Committed, Loving,
yet Asexual Relationships' on the once-popular online communicative network Usenet. B's post was made near the dawn
of the so-called Information Age – an era when digital sharing
and communication, although initially quite cumbersome,
was becoming more accessible to certain subsets of the 'general public,' who were usually middle to upper class.
Newfound access to networks like Usenet meant that some
members of certain groups on the social periphery could reach
wider audiences with greater ease.

Usenet was organized into various newsgroups, each
intended for text-based communication surrounding a particular topic or theme. Discussion occurred in a manner similar
to email, although with less privacy, and newsgroup topics
ranged from political discourse to popular subcultures, similar
to how discussion forums operate on the internet. B thought

soc.couples – frequented by others seeking relationship advice – was a suitable place to discuss their concerns. In their post, B explained that their asexuality (defined differently from the contemporary definition of asexuality) made them feel isolated from the sexual world around them. They stated feeling as if the majority of others around them would never marry "a person who doesn't want sex." As a result, B posed the question whether others thought them to be "an extreme minority" or if they had a high likelihood of finding a spouse.[2] Although B expressed concern over this personal matter, no discontentment was directed at their asexuality: "For those people who want to call into question my asexuality, please don't! Yes, I've tried sex. I know what I'm saying 'no' to."[3] The first reply B received was from a user who will be referred to here as D, who expressed that they admired B's courage to "be yourself when that runs counter to the 'norm'."[4] D also supported B's assertion that the possibility of finding a 'committed, loving, yet asexual' relationship would indeed be a difficult task. As such, they suggested that it was the parameters B established which constrained the possibility of forming such a relationship. However, rather than diminish or downplay B's experience as unreasonable, D supported B's desire to form a relationship despite the challenges of overcoming such obstacles.

The second response was from K, who emphasized how B's predicament was a "tricky situation" and explained in considerable depth how they thought B could approach the issue of forming an 'asexual' relationship. K believed that there could be a large number of potential spouses for B and suggested that they try advertising.[5] K also explored some of the practical difficulties that asexual people may encounter when navigating relationship formation. They considered the possibility of different relationships manifesting between asexual and non-asexual people, stating that there should be no issue with such arrangements so long as all parties involved understand that the needs of everyone involved are being met.[6]

Finally, another user, P, expressed some distrust in B's asexual identity. They suggested that B continue trying to locate a person who would open them to sexual experiences. P mentioned how some people may have "Victorian purist ideas" deeply embedded within them that restrict them from sexual intimacy, although specified that they were not including B within that group.[7] The mention here of Victorian ideals is noteworthy, even though P claims that it is not directed at B. While it is true that Victorian ideals have played a role in conditioning many people to adopt 'conservative' stances toward sexuality, asexuality itself is not simply a byproduct of the indoctrination of Victorian ideals in regard to notions of purity. This is an assumption that non-asexual people can sometimes make: that aces are prudish or are simply choosing to abstain from sexual activity. P reflected this attitude as follows:

> what you think is asexuality could actually be just the reaction to not having found the right person. [. . .] It can happen that you find a person who will bring to rise the appetite for sex even in you.[8]

As I read through B's thread posted in 1990, I resonated with the feeling of being isolated as an asexual person in a sexual world in my own life, navigating a world in which sex has come to be imbued with more meaning than it probably should. Sometimes I find myself feeling like B, suddenly pondering the logistics of relationship formation despite the hurdles I would be tasked with overcoming, while other times it is of no concern to me. I have encountered many aces who, like B, express their desire to form a relationship yet remain concerned about the viability of fulfilling such a desire. I have encountered just as many aces who are simply uninterested in forming a relationship altogether. This is because aces are a diverse group of people, and their *relationship* to relationships is not monolithic.

Although P seems to be genuinely well intentioned in their lengthy reply, there are several issues with replies like these that warrant closer scrutiny. As Chapter 1 discussed, many people today often interpret asexuality to be conditional. In 1990, B anticipated a response such as P's before it came, indicating how attitudes toward asexuality have not shifted much in the decades since this post. P's response suggested that they knew an asexual person's life better than the asexual person themselves, making asexuality out to be a byproduct of sexual solitude – a mask that, whether consciously or not, is worn until the 'right person' comes along. When asexuality is understood as a symptom, rectifying its source becomes a 'cure,' even if doing so reinforces the expectation that an asexual person must pursue 'Mx. Right' until they are found. Despite B's postscript, P seemed more willing to urge them to keep *pursuing* rather than to accept asexuality.

A few days later, B posted a short follow-up message thanking respondents and, as a goodbye, wrote: "Most of the responses were very encouraging! I've come away feeling much more optimistic!"[9] B's 1990 post reveals much about perceptions of asexuality prior to the World Wide Web, providing us with a window to reflect on what has and hasn't changed, and with what effects.

A Decentralized Identity

In the 1990s, asexuality existed in a relatively decentralized form. Without a widely accepted definition, the term was used to represent a variety of different experiences, many of which addressed some form of sexual or sexuality-related absence. We can visualize this by referring to the image of a peg and a hole. When an identity is centralized, we are the pegs working to fit into established or centralized holes. The contours of the hole have been carved out and we categorize ourselves as fitting within them. When an identity is decentralized, the agency to shape the hole around ourselves is ours.

There are pros and cons in each scenario. Centralized identities may be perceived as more practical because they result in the formation of a tidy system of identity organization. When a person refers to themselves as asexual, aromantic, or agender, they can be more quickly understood by a centralized definition. There is less space for confusion or misunderstanding. There is also more ease in identifying or studying a population. Centralized identities are more apt to be imposed from a dominant worldview onto another. While a decentralized identity leaves space open for interpretation and elasticity, a centralized identity leaves little liminal space. This system, in which each identity box can be precisely labeled and differentiated, may risk reinforcing a single worldview as universal 'truth.' At the same time, identities that remain too decentralized may become understood as useless, mired with confusion whenever surfacing in conversation. Decentralization may also leave open more space for centralization to take place under the direction of influential insiders or co-option by outsiders to the community who can alter social understandings of an identity for a particular agenda.

A 1993 Usenet discussion thread entitled 'I'm asexual!' on newsgroup soc.bi — a space for discussion centered on bisexuality — exemplifies how asexuality functioned in its decentralized form. The post was authored by a user referred to here as S who identified as asexual using an analogy of *tone* and *volume*:

> Think of 'tone' as the knob that describes your orientation . . . one way is heterosexual, the other way is homosexual. [. . .] The other knob, the 'volume' knob, describes how powerfully one feels that sexual orientation. This has nothing to do with libido . . . that's another amplifier entirely. [. . .] You see, my volume knob is set to zero. [. . .] And when the volume is turned down so it can't be heard, does it really matter what the tone is set to?[10]

S adopted an uncharacteristic approach to asexual identity, defining it as a lack of feeling one's orientation. Attempting to clarify exactly what S meant by 'feeling' one's orientation is difficult. At one point S provided the examples of Pat Robertson (based on the Christian broadcaster's overtly homophobic and conservative views) and Harvey Fierstein (based on the playwright and actor's 'effeminate' gender expression and 'flamboyant' personality) as people who apparently 'feel' their 'opposing' orientations (hetero vs. homo) or 'tones' ('bass' and 'treble') respectively. There is evidently intended to be some humor and sarcasm in S's framing, which makes the post's inclusion in asexual history somewhat dubious (although it is included here largely because of the conversations it provoked).

In their concluding remarks, S suggests that asexuality is present when a person just feels in a general sense, but does not direct their feelings into what may be considered stereotypical behavior associated with intensely heterosexual or homosexual expression. Although likely unintentional, given their definition of asexuality, I find S's model intriguing because it frames asexuality as overlapping with other sexual identities. Rather than being presented as an additional tone setting, S situate asexuality as part of the 'volume' setting that exists independently of tone. While this is probably attributed to S's definition of asexuality as a lack of feeling one's orientation, elsewhere in their post they mentioned how other elements of one's sexuality may also exist as separate from the tone setting as another amplifier or 'set of knobs,' so it may not be too far a stretch to say that sexual attraction and sexual desire could hypothetically function as one of these additional devices. With a little tweaking, S's model could function as a framework to explain how asexuality may overlap with one's orientation. This is relevant because asexuality is sometimes still discussed as an entirely separate orientation, rather than as potentially overlapping with other orientations.

Unsurprisingly, given the ambiguous humor of the post, several users responded with confusion, not just at S's uncharacteristic definition of asexuality, but also at the concept of asexuality itself. One user chimed in that S might be more appropriately considered confused rather than asexual. Another user explained that asexuality more accurately could be described as a total absence of attraction to anyone. Respondent J wrote that S was not asexual just because they did not identify or 'feel' their orientation, finding this framing to be preposterous. They expressed how asexuality was more appropriately defined as "a lack of sexuality."[11] More than just a series of replies, this discussion thread thus illustrated some of the ways in which asexual identity was understood prior to its centralization.

J themself also expressed how labels or identities are socially constructed and not essential to human experience, arguing that departing from the label-oriented system is a valid approach to navigating identity, a sentiment shared by respondent M, who also indicated their desire to move away from labels in their response to S's post:

> the search for a sufficiently broad label is doomed to fail, since any new label will quickly gain a stereotype set to match [. . .] Thus the solution is to trash the whole restrictive labelling system, by not allowing a label to restrict your activities.[12]

M mentioned that an approach that disregards the pursuit of labels entirely may be more useful or preferable than *misapplying* asexuality to represent an experience of 'not feeling' an orientation. As a result, M suggested that the entire labeling system be discarded, moving away from allowing labels to police our behavior. Instead of attempting to fit or restrict our experiences to labels, their post suggests that we should focus on being ourselves and use labels when convenient or fruitful, rather than using them to overcomplicate ourselves in words or restrict our imaginations and experiences.

Overall, M's post can be read as a commentary on the nature of labels and the transition from decentralization to centralization. M implied that the process of labeling will become more and more specified, seeming to foreshadow the transition of asexual identity from decentralized to a more centralized identity as well as the emergence of so-called microlabels that are used to identify more and more specific permutations of our experiences.

About a week after this thread, another user, G, opened a new topic addressing S's discussion post, remarking that "all this talk about some people being 'asexual'" was leading them to question if asexual people had a place online to discuss their experiences. User C responded by imagining what a hypothetical asexual community would discuss. Conjuring up a hypothetical scenario, C wrote: "How can you masturbate and still call yourself an asexual? You're disgusting!"[13] This hypothetical comment reflected how C believed that an asexual community would engage in self-policing or gatekeeping of asexual identity to exclude or invalidate others due to their disconformity from the 'true' definition of asexuality.

Another user, T, dismissed C's cynicism, writing: "I don't really find it that funny," and wrote that an asexual community could find many important topics to discuss. For T, these topics included how to navigate being "asexual in a world so obsessed with sexuality," challenges in regard to relationships, and wondering if what they referred to as "asexual romance" could exist.[14] T thus imagined an asexual community that would broadly discuss how to navigate the sexual expectations of society and relationships, rather than be concerned with intracommunal gatekeeping. T's questioning of 'asexual romance' also foreshadows the creation of aromantic identity.

Overall, these discussion threads posted on Usenet in the early 1990s illustrate how asexuality, in its decentralized form, was open to some degree of debate regarding its specific definition. However, although users debated understandings of asexuality, what remained relatively uniform was the association between asexuality and some form of *absence*, *lacking*, or estrangement from human emotion or *feeling*.

I'll be your robot, honey
Sour not sweet
I guess I'll never be complete
By your standards of who I 'should be'
Out of commission: missing parts
Inside this hardened shell of skin
But aren't we all just picking up
The pieces of who we 'should be'
. . . honey?

The Asexual Abyss

Although these posts are from the early 1990s, the assumption that asexuality is marked by 'frigid' or 'robotic' behavior remains pervasive today. Catherine Clifford commented on this in an article for *AZE*:

> Many of us [asexual people] have internalized words like 'cold' and 'frigid,' usually hurled at us in insult. These corpse-like adjectives assume that our bodies aren't alive, that somehow we fail to be fully human.[15]

In another article for *AZE* that reflected on some aspects that define asexual culture, one often shared experience was being referred to as robotic.[16] A WebMD article similarly noted that aroaces are especially subject to assumptions of being "cold and robotic."[17]

The perception that asexuality is represented through being devoid of humanity – implied in the association with roboticism – has been deeply reinforced in media representations. However, there have been some recent attempts to challenge this narrative.[18] In a piece for *AZE* titled 'Asexual Positivity in a Game About Sexy Demons,' Alex Henderson discussed how online dating simulator *Cute Demon Crashers* by Sugarscript opens space for positive asexual representation:

> Most other fiction seemingly runs on the principle that *of course* you want to [have or pursue sex] [. . .] If that wanting never appears, the character [in most other fiction] is likely a villainous or humorous husk of a human being, meant to be Othered whether that's for horror or for laughs – or simply waiting for the right person to thaw their unnatural frigidity.[19]

As Henderson states, the asexual-coded character is commonly *Othered* or portrayed as inherently abnormal in some respect. Jessica Vazquez similarly commented on this Othering of asexual- and aromantic-coded characters in an article for Autostraddle, citing several potential examples of asexual representation, including character Parvati Holcomb in the action role-playing game *The Outer Worlds* (2019). Although Holcomb is not explicitly identified as *asexual*, Vazquez argues that there are moments in the game that reflect ace experiences, such as Holcomb's line, "I'm not much interested in physical stuff. Never have been. Leastways not like other folk seem to be. It's not that I can't? I just don't care for it." This form of non-explicit asexual representation can be just as important in contributing to a cultural shift as named representation:

If you're looking for an example of how to speak to an asexual audience even when your characters aren't ace, this kind
of dialog is important. Sending the message that you can be
loved without having sex with someone you're in a relationship [with] is an important message to send especially to a
younger audience.[20]

Despite the recent uptick in media representations that challenge domineering sexual expectations, allonormativity (the
assumption that everyone experiences sexual attraction) still
remains pervasive. How can we deconstruct the powerful
grip this assumption may have in our lives?

Staring into the asexual abyss revealed to me the ways in
which sexuality is deeply entwined with notions of being
human under colonial cisheteropatriarchy. The abyss is the
shadow realm where what is supposedly not possible still
exists. It is in those unintelligible spaces of existence, detached
from that which is assumed to be natural, that we become in
tune with our humanity.

How then to harness the power of the abyss? It is to know
that if I am nothing but a blackhole to you, that I should own
my ability to confound your imagination; be the enigma and
take the power to diminish my existence away from you?
This act of reclaiming one's displacement from normalcy has
been framed as a pathway toward self-empowerment by many
who have been ostracized. Self-identified asexual people in
the 1990s used reclamation of the abyss as a tactic to organize
a community by refusing dominant narratives regarding what
it means to be human and on the purpose of life.

By the late 1990s, discussions of asexual identity online had
transitioned from Usenet to the World Wide Web, which utilized webpages rather than newsgroups as an interface. On May

30, 1997, 'My Life as an Amoeba' by Zoe O'Reilly was one of the earliest articles on asexuality published on the Web via AZStarNet.com (affiliated with the *Arizona Daily Star* newspaper). In the article, O'Reilly reclaimed the association between asexuality and the non-human through the figure of the amoeba. Other groups, such as the Haven for the Human Amoeba founded in 2000, would similarly exhibit this embrace. Amoebas are unicellular organisms that hold the ability to change shape and reproduce through a form of asexual reproduction, in which it splits through binary fission. O'Reilly embraced this comparison to frame the article's discussion:

> In this time of teen mothers and raging hormones, my people should be praised for being what we are. Me, the amoeba, the androgynous Pat (from *Saturday Night Live*). Our lives aren't dedicated to reproducing the latest bizarre love triangle on *Melrose Place*.[21]

O'Reilly approached asexual identity, which was referred to in the article as being absent of sexuality, from an angle that presented it even as a morally preferable alternative to a sex-crazed society. At the same time, she wrote that she was not self-righteous enough to make this aspect of herself into a means of getting attention.[22]

On the subject of who was and was not asexual, O'Reilly seemed to embrace the decentralized approach, referring to Renée Descartes' philosophical principle 'I think, therefore I am' to argue that anyone who thinks of themselves as asexual is, in fact, asexual.[23] Historically, the phrase 'I think therefore I am' emerged in the Enlightenment period to replace the idea of the 'transcendental God'; a turn away from theocracy and the 'Great Chain of Being' that had prevailed throughout the

Medieval European era. With the destabilization of the 'transcendental God' at the top of the hierarchy, the European human-subject now assumed the role of a 'rational', 'Godlike' figure. This philosophical shift motivated the European human-subject to believe that it held the "capacity to determine for itself its own laws" and, by extension, the laws of others.[24] In other words, the human-subject not only assumed a right to define itself, but to define those who it deemed itself to be superior to – imposing its worldview (of which identity is a part) onto others. From the perspective of the 'rational' thinker, such a phrase was understood as liberating; as a triumph of the human over primitivity.

O'Reilly's invocation of the phrase was also expressed as a liberatory statement, though in a different context. Here, it was used to encourage people who may feel lost or devoid to define for themselves a sense of belonging, which in this case could be found through asexual identity, based on their capacity to make such judgment, since, from this perspective, so long as a person thinks they are asexual, they *are* asexual.

O'Reilly's decentralized approach brought people together who found resonance with the term *asexual* as a way of describing their experiences. She concluded her article by reflecting on how asexual identity could proliferate further through a kind of recruitment of new members.[25] I imagine that, in this context, recruiting people to identify as asexual would mean spreading awareness of the term's existence in a manner so that those who feel resonance with *asexual* might learn to identify with it. The beginnings of this growing population seemed to be reflected in the lively discussion that occurred in the comments section of O'Reilly's article, an unprecedented phenomenon in the cyberspatial emergence of asexual identity.

The Centralization of Asexual Identity

The roots of the centralization of asexual identity began as more and more asexual people came together to express their perspectives. While this initially began on Usenet, it gained traction with the shift in popularity to the World Wide Web. The comments section of O'Reilly's article served as a meeting place for asexual people to step out of isolation, and many comments thanked O'Reilly as a result. Some of the comments spoke of O'Reilly's article being the first place they had seen their own experiences and concerns reflected. Other commenters expressed appreciation about finding any information on their identity being written about online and reflected on their past encounters with invalidating narratives, noting how they had to assert that their lives were still fulfilling despite others mocking or pitying them.[26]

The comments on O'Reilly's article illustrated how early online networks, whether on Usenet or in the comments sections of Web articles, connected people who otherwise may have struggled to bond over their shared identities and experiences. The digital space therefore provided them with avenues toward reaching the important understanding that they were not alone in the world.

It also provided non-asexual people with a window into asexual experiences, who may have otherwise never encountered them in person or the idea of asexuality at all. Comments sections allowed non-asexuals not only an opportunity to witness, but to engage by expressing their perspectives on the identity directly to asexual people in a more public and lasting way. For O'Reilly's article, this included supporters who expressed admiration and even envy toward asexual people for their disentanglement from what they saw as some of the burdens that sexual attraction and desire could bring into people's lives. They expressed encouraging words toward asexual people for their courage to be themselves in a society that they identified as being overly focused on sex.[27]

Responses from non-asexual people also included the familiar skepticism from critics who spoke of asexuality as a *dampener* on the 'true' potential of what life has to offer. One commenter, for instance, framed asexuality as a limitation to growing in life, claiming that the identity blocks one's capacity to connect with others in an intimate or loving way. This, they argued, positioned asexuality as an exemplification of humanity's modern disconnection with nature.[28] While I agree with the premise that the modern/colonial world is defined by seeing ourselves as fundamentally disconnected from nature, I do not see asexual identity as exemplifying this point, but rather things like the mass destruction of environments and extraction of 'resources' in the pursuit of maximizing corporate profits. People can simultaneously believe in the interconnectedness of all things – recognizing that humans are interconnected with nature – yet also understand that we are complex and diverse beings who may simply use different labels or words to help us communicate and understand each other.

Not every person was put on this planet to be the same or live through the same experiences. Some people may experience low levels (or none at all) of sexual attraction, sexual desire, or sexual drive, while others may experience high levels (what is low and high is relative to cultural or social standards). Diversity is an important factor to the surviving and thriving of life, even if that is for reasons we cannot immediately understand. Asexual people are sometimes considered unnatural because they are assumed not to be naturally inclined toward procreation. I have encountered many people in my life who believe that heterosexuality is inherently procreative and is thus the only 'natural' expression of sexuality. It occurs to me to ask the question: When did we become so confident in ourselves that we began to believe that we could speak for nature? That we could tell its secrets or reveal its complexity? That we could classify some of its beings as unnatural and others as natural?

i have thoughts sometimes about having sex
the pleasure
the pain
wondering what meaning it would give me
that others claim i am missing
would it fill me with the life
i have supposedly never known
leave me suspended in a new
kind of absence
would it give me answers to questions
i am no longer asking
i am no longer asking

The comment stream on O'Reilly's article included a reply by David Jay, the founder of AVEN, who notified commenters of a new online asexual community that could be found at asexuality.org.[29] O'Reilly's article was thus a critical touchstone for the emergence and growth of asexual communities online, since it operated as an early hub for asexual people to branch out from.

AVEN would go on to become the central online space for

aces and play a crucial role in the centralization of asexual identity. Operating via the URL asexuality.org, AVEN established itself as a leading voice on asexual identity, coalesced around a now uniform definition. This was listed at the top of the AVEN forum in August 2002: "*Asexual: A person who does not experience sexual attraction.*" The forum at this time had forty-one members,[30] while in 2023 it surpassed 150,000 members. Indicating the intent behind starting a community for asexual people, the website included the following explanation: "Unlike gay, lesbian and bisexual people[,] asexual people are not compelled by sexual attraction to seek each other out, which has made it more difficult for us to build a community." AVEN listed a variety of hypothetical questions and answers about asexuality on its FAQ page, including "Can asexual people fall in love? Do asexual people have a sex drive? Are you sexually repressed? Is it possible that you just haven't found the right person yet?" among others.[31] AVEN's formation in the early 2000s was forged with the ambition to address many of the same challenges that aces encounter today.

By February 2003, AVEN had added a FAQ subpage entitled 'Questions Asked by Asexual and Questioning People.'[32] The page organized hypothetical questions regarding asexuality into sections, such as the definition of asexuality, concerns over 'fitting in' within the community, and inquiries about asexual relationships. The response to the question "Am I asexual?" included:

Remember that the definition of asexuality is "No or low sexual attraction to other people". Of course, just because you fit this definition doesn't mean you have to identify as asexual. That's your decision.[33]

The general tone of the page was inclusive and focused on spreading awareness about asexuality through informative and well-detailed responses. In one response, the author wrote: "There is no hierarchy of asexuality" along with the statements that "Asexuals with romance drives are not 'less asexual' than those without" and "Asexuals who are in sexual relationships with loving partners have as much value in the community as those who have never had a single sexual experience."[34] The author thus made it clear that there was diversity within the asexual community that should be both recognized and validated.

At the same time, the importance of using a precise definition of asexuality was evidently important. In their response to "I find people attractive and I get horny but I dislike sex and would never do it, am I asexual?," their phrasing on what constituted asexuality was clear:

> If you're turned on by other people then you don't fit the definition. [. . .] Asexuals do not get horny toward other people, they would feel completely satisfied if they never shared a single sexual experience for the rest of their lives.[35]

This response demonstrates a shift toward centralization in comparison to the early days of Usenet where asexuality could be many things to many different people. By the early 2000s, asexuality was becoming a more centralized term with a more specific definition. Classifying who was and was not asexual had thus become a part of asexual discourse.

Conclusion

While it is arguably not the main purpose of identity centralization to exclude or ostracize, this appears to become an
inevitable byproduct, even on a small scale, since people who
do not define their identity to the ascending specified definition may not perfectly 'fit' into the box that is being
established. This is not to say that identity centralization is
inherently a 'bad' thing, just that it can come to exclude those
who may not conform to its standardization. Balancing centralization and decentralization by forming an identity around
several core ideas, beliefs, or understandings that are not too
constricting or limiting, while also retaining the identity's
'use' as a collective label to organize around, may be a beneficial approach – inclusive 'where it counts' and exclusive 'where
it doesn't' – although reaching such a place is riddled with
complex obstacles.

The various people who were self-identifying as asexual
on Usenet in the 1990s did not each define their asexuality as
a lack of sexual attraction. As a result, with centralization, they
may have come to be excluded from the emerging identity
and subsequent community that they themselves played a
role in forming. It is important not to forget this, even if we
can also recognize the benefits of identity centralization
within the Western system, which requires categorization
and clearly definable boundaries to acquire 'legitimacy.' The
everyday invalidation that asexual people endure as a result
of the proliferation of the narrative that everyone should
inherently experience sexual attraction is a worthy challenge
to overcome. Actualizing the objective to validate one's asexual identity is therefore to fight against social isolation and

ostracization that emerges from being told your experience is 'impossible' or 'unnatural.'

After having chronicled the early emergence of asexual identity in cyberspace, I do not speak against centralization, but rather recognize that it may be an important part of working toward social awareness and, hopefully, more understanding and increased wellbeing for people whose experiences have been pathologized or made invisible in the modern colonial world. At the same time, I remain mindful of more expansive imaginings of asexuality, historically and presently, even when they do not perfectly conform to the manifestations of centralization. This is because, in general, such imaginings keep us conscious of possibilities beyond the lines that have been drawn. It is such a simultaneous recognition that remains crucial to hold in more ways than one.

What comes forth and what is lost
In the emergence
Is sometimes unforeseen
Until long after it has passed
Until the words we use have changed
Until our tongues have been tied
And we are drowning
In the memories
Illusions failing
Hollowed tunnel vision
Leads us to remember
That the birth of one reality
Could be the death of another

4

Victorian Desirelessness and (Un)civilized Desires

On December 11, 1860, four months prior to the outbreak of the American Civil War, Dr. William Alexander Hammond privately consulted with a 33-year-old man whom he described in *Sexual Impotence in the Male*, published in 1884, as "strong, well-built, and apparently healthy." Hammond referred to this man as Mr. W and reported that he had asked for a consultation to "ascertain if anything could be done for him." Hammond's concern came after hearing that, despite persistent effort, Mr. W had "never experienced the slightest desire for sexual intercourse nor any venereal excitement." Mr. W reportedly told Hammond that he had come to him with hopes that "in the resources of medicine there might be something that would alter his nature so as to make sexual intercourse possible to him."[1]

Hammond was a leading physician by the mid-nineteenth century who had previously served in the US army and had just accepted a professorship of anatomy and physiology at the University of Maryland Medical School.[2] He would go on to serve in the American Civil War as the eleventh Surgeon General of the United States from 1862 to 1864 and produce several medical texts pathologizing various diseases and conditions of the body.[3] This included *Sexual Impotence*, in which Hammond cited Mr. W as a patient case study of innate sexual desirelessness. Labeling this patient case effectively transformed an experience that has presumably always been present in humanity into a new medical classification to be studied as an allegedly unnatural deficiency of the human condition.

Hammond defined impotence as the lack of sexual desire related "altogether to the act of intercourse" and classified sexual desirelessness as a unique defect in male sexual performance separate from other forms of impotence. Hammond referred to it officially as an "original absence of all sexual desire" and documented the cases of two men who exemplified this condition since birth (one of them being Mr. W). While Hammond recognized that this new categorization of a perceived sexual deficiency only applied to a minor subset of the population, he emphasized that "there are persons in apparent good health who have never experienced sexual desires."[4] Hammond also documented two women whom he felt reflected this condition – Mrs. C and Mrs. O – in *Sexual Impotence in the Male and Female* (1887). Hammond likely considered these patients unique because their sexual desirelessness could not be attributed to an anatomical or biological inability to perform sexual intercourse – subjects of later chapters in *Sexual Impotence* – but rather was deemed to be without perceptible cause.

Hammond referred to this categorization as a fundamentally new and unexplored endeavor that diverted from the work of his peers in the medical field. For instance, while he noted in *Sexual Impotence* that French physician Félix Roubaud had previously hypothesized the possibility of frigidity since birth and without perceptible cause, he wrote that "Roubaud expresses doubt regarding the existence of idiopathic [unexplainable] absence of sexual desire" and had "always found the cause to exist either in moral circumstances or in general or local conditions affecting the generative apparatus." Hammond further remarked that Roubaud was unable "to discover them [those who lacked sexual desire without perceptible cause] in the writings of others."[5] His motivation for addressing Roubaud may have stemmed from his belief in "aggressive materialism," as he professed that it was "extremely important that a theory should be 'based upon facts'" and be observable in the material world, hence his rigorous study of patient cases.[6]

In the late nineteenth century, studies on human sexuality were budding. Hammond was "a leading specialist in sexual disorders" whose perspective on sexual desire established him as a major figure in sexology.[7] Hammond himself believed that sexual desire was instinctive, declaring that "there are various circumstances which to these exert an influence in abolishing the natural sexual desire of the individual."[8] Sexologists of the late 1800s utilized scientific discourse to attempt to define the 'laws of sexuality' and, in turn, normalized the medical study of sexuality and gender. Among these rules was the belief that human beings are born with an inherent hetero-oriented sexual desire, which was then "popularized by an army of sex advice writers"[9] and ascended into the public consciousness as truth. This is how sexologists shaped the sexual and gendered culture of the West and, as a result of colonialism, the world.

Hammond's discussion on sexual desirelessness marked its transition from an uncategorized phenomenon into a newly classifiable state of being. Desirelessness was not only pathologized through sexology discourses as deviant in its divergence from the dominant sexual and gendered expectations of sexologists, but also in its undetectable nature, its inability to be perceptively marked upon the body. It is in the latter that desirelessness holds a uniquely subversive potential to critique and deconstruct hegemonic norms of gender, sex, and sexual desire from within the veil of presumed 'heterosexuality.' However, as the narratives of Hammond's patients will show, those who embodied desirelessness internalized themselves to be broken and sought compliance with Victorian social expectations. Their conformist actions suggest that the subversive potential of desirelessness may only be realized through satisfaction in one's absence of sexual desire despite prevailing social expectations – to be content in embodying what has been categorically produced against what is perceived as natural. It is this act that may encourage the reorientation of social norms.

Rather than attempting to misapply desirelessness as a historical representation of asexuality, I am more interested in exploring what those who embodied desirelessness over a hundred years ago can teach us about what it means to live in opposition to the dominant sexual and gendered expectations today. Examining desirelessness in Victorian America may also function as an exercise in what Ela Przybylo and Danielle Cooper theorize as "asexual 'resonances' – or traces, touches, instances" within a larger asexual archival project.[10] This can prompt a critical reflection of how 'the science of sexuality' was constructed through medical discourse, through witnessing the implications of such conditioning on real people. The discussion is reframed here from the perspectives of the patients, rather than the medical institution, in order to break from reproducing dominant narratives.

I take this approach to reframe the historical narrative differently than is accounted for in medical journals of the period – which are oriented through the lens of the dominant gaze upheld by the physician or sexologist in question. As Patti Duncan states, "It is by small acts and insights that change occurs, through a process of critical remembering [. . .] We begin to alter history."[11] How we remember the past holds the power to alter the present. Destabilizing the master narratives can therefore open up possibilities to imagine things differently and see from vantage points we would never have considered or that we were told were simply not worthy of our consideration.

The fragments left behind
Scattered indications of lives
Reflected in time
Remains pushing forward
Like some crowded destiny
Calling across time
I hear their cries
And so I try

Desireless Manhood: The Case of Mr. W

Upon his arrival at Hammond's office in 1860, Mr. W indicated that he sought a consultation in an effort to make "sexual intercourse possible to him, even if the development of desire were out of the question." Mr. W reported that his attempts to forcibly stimulate sexual desire instead inspired a strong repugnant reaction towards sex and when "attempts were persevered with, nausea and vomiting, accompanied with nervous and physical prostration, ensued." When Mr. W attempted to "excite desire by imagining erotic scenes of various kinds," Hammond indicated that he produced erections, but that "there was no desire." Rather, "on the contrary, feelings of repugnance and disgust were at once excited."[12] Mr. W's ambition to inspire sexual desire despite his repulsion of it demonstrates the depth at which he had problematized himself. Philosopher Michel Foucault wrote about discursive power:[13] how the writings of sexologists produced and proliferated the notion of 'non-normative' sexual behaviors while simultaneously normalizing the monogamous heterosexual couple under the authority of medical discourse.[14] It was this discursive power that motivated people like Mr. W to approach Hammond and other sexologists in the pursuit of self-correction.

The emergence of medical discourse concerning patients in a similar condition to Mr. W was not unique in the period. In *Psychopathia Sexualis*, first published in 1886, Austro-German sexologist Richard von Krafft-Ebing provided a summation of fellow clinicians who wrote on phenomena similar to what he himself classified as 'anaesthesia sexualis,' or the absence of sexual feeling as a congenital human anomaly (being present from birth). Krafft-Ebing wrote how those who could be categorized under this distinction were "functionally sexless individuals [who] are seldom seen, and are, indeed, always persons having degenerative defects, and in whom other functional cerebral disturbances, states of psychical degeneration, and even anatomical signs of degeneration, are observed." He then cited patient cases of French psychiatrist Henri Legrand du Saulle along with Hammond's patients as "pure cases" that reflected anaesthesia sexualis.[15] His discussion exhibited how both European and American sexological discourse played a role in pathologizing desirelessness – a transnational origins moment in Western medical practice.

As a lack of sexual desire was categorized as abnormal by

sexologists, a new pathology emerged. This was a trend among medical practitioners in Western societies, who began extensively recording and classifying people's sexual practices and pleasures. Certain expressions were medicalized as deficient, while others became indulgent or excessive. Therefore, as this discourse designated what was abnormal, it also defined the boundaries of what was considered normal.[16] On the ground level, this introduced discursive pressures into people's everyday lives. Living amidst this emerging discourse, people such as Mr. W were conditioned to understand themselves as both sexually unnatural and, by extension, gender deviant.

Hammond organized *Sexual Impotence* in gendered terms and believed that the issue of impotence was more important in men than it was in women.[17] This was noted by scholars Peter Cryle and Alison Moore:

> So when Hammond announced in the second (1887) edition of his book that he had now modified the first of 1884, 'related only to impotence in the male', by adding a section on women, the standard order of priorities was untroubled. Women patients were literally an afterthought in this context [. . .] In a sense, Hammond's work offers one of the strongest examples of the 'one-sex model' at work even at the end of the nineteenth century [. . .] insisting that men and women could be spoken about in much the same terms.[18]

Although Hammond's work exhibited a one-sex model, a two-sex model that stressed unique differences between men and women – a *binary sex system* and a subsequent *binary two-gender system* – had already supplanted the one-sex model by the early nineteenth century.[19]

As the gendered roles for men and women were redefined through the prism of the two-sex model, men's and women's social worlds were increasingly policed and the two genders became highly segregated.[20] Hammond's patients navigated an increasingly two-sexed world where the lines between what was considered appropriate masculine and feminine behavior grew sharper and more complex. Central to this intensely gendered division between men and women were behaviors related to sexual desire. Men were expected to have strong sexual desires for women and women were expected to have reciprocal service-based sexual desires for men, although there was less consensus on the acceptable amount of desire for women in the 1800s.[21]

Mr. W, who lacked sexual desire and was repulsed by sex, navigated Victorian life in opposition to his gendered role upheld by the two-sex world he inhabited. Sexual expectations placed upon white middle-class men, presumably like Mr. W,[22] entwined masculinity with the expectation of an overpowering sex drive. Unlike women, Victorian men were said to be "beset by powerful gusts of sinful sexual desires" that functioned as the source of both their societal danger and power.[23]

Sexologists such as Hammond professed that men were *naturally* sexually aggressive individuals who 'justifiably' required an outlet to release their dangerous sexual passions, which became the duty of their submissive wives. Louise Hardwick argued that sexual aggression in men was naturalized in sexological literature even to the degree that it was deemed an appropriate explanation for necrophilia among men.[24]

With the normalization of this idea, manliness became defined by one's ability to exhibit restraint and mastery over one's sexual desires. White men used this definition of manliness to refer to themselves as superior to those "less manly than himself – whether [that be] his wife, his children, his employ-ees, or his racial 'inferiors.'"[25]

At the same time, a core component of this definition of manliness was the expression of dominant sexual expressions in marriage. Mr. W's own aspirations for marriage were enmeshed within this context, likely complicated by the expectation that "powerful sexual passion was an intrinsic part of a loving marriage and demonstrated forceful virility and strong manliness."[26] Hammond recorded Mr. W's concerns in the following passage:

There were many reasons why this gentleman should marry. There was a considerable property held in trust for any chil-dren he might have, but which without offspring of his [own] would go from his family partly to people strangers to him and partly to certain charitable institutions. And again, strange as it may seem, he liked the companionship of women and was anxious to have a home of his own, and a wife with whom he might at least associate in a platonic way. In his present condition, he felt that all these things were impossible.[27]

Mr. W not only felt separated from marriage because of this sexual expectation, but as a consequence had no way of access-ing the legal privileges unequally afforded to men in marriage, including control of inheritance.[28] Although Mr. W expressed his desire to form a platonic relationship, he may have deter-mined that it would be impossible to form a relationship in this way because of the dominant expectations.

Victorian men who fulfilled or released their sexual passions outside of marriage through "masturbation, commercial sex [. . .] or other illicit sexual activities" were also marked in the dominant public social script as demonstrating masculine weakness.[29] However, regardless of this moral stigma, many Victorian men did engage in these so-called unmanly pursuits, demonstrated via the presence of vice districts within every American metropolis that catered to an illegalized yet permissible male-focused sexual desire.[30] Hammond recorded that Mr. W admitted to reading "libidinous books" and associating "with lewd women" to attempt to generate venereal excitations and produce sexual desire.[31] While participation in illicit sexual activities urged some men to question their morality and potential unmanliness, this was often rectified by the sexist authority afforded to men within marriage to unquestionably exert their sexual desires onto their wives. Despite Mr. W's attempt to cultivate sexual desire by associating with women who frequented vice districts, Hammond recorded that his engagement in this practice proved to be unsuccessful and only resulted in "his repugnance [of sex] increasing."[32]

Mr. W's sex repulsion prevented him from stimulating sexual desire through forced action or "lewd" association, which prompted him to consider the vice of masturbation as an alternative way to garner sexual pleasure. Hammond recorded that Mr. W considered whether there "might be pleasure in masturbation" after another failed attempt at sexual intercourse at the age of twenty-two. However, despite openly professing his considerations to masturbate, Hammond recorded that Mr. W was "very emphatic in declaring that he had never indulged in this vice," noting that his body language while discussing masturbation was "frank in the extreme." Hammond wrote that he had "no reason to doubt the truth of his [Mr. W's] declaration."[33]

Mr. W's fervent denial of his participation in the act again demonstrates the role of Victorian views toward sexual expression outside of the dominant-husband-submissive-wife dynamic in marriage. Victorian men like Mr. W were conditioned to fear masturbation as precipitating insanity and to believe "that nocturnal seminal 'leakage' could kill them."[34] More than religion, this social conditioning relied on Victorian medical discourses for legitimacy.[35] Talk of a "masturbation hysteria" was promoted in numerous medical journals published in the period and shaped wider social attitudes toward the practice.[36] In such a social climate, Mr. W was conditioned to deny any engagement in masturbation, which could have otherwise been a pleasurable practice for him. The lack of outlets may have further contributed to Mr. W seeking correction by appealing to the same institution that pathologized him as defective, although this is unclear. Hammond advised that "it might be possible for him to accomplish the sexual act notwithstanding the disgust, the faintness, the nausea and vomiting, and by perseverance to overcome the idiosyncrasy." Yet, despite Mr. W's previous efforts to satisfy the standards of male sexual normalcy via repeated action, he departed from his consultation with Hammond, still promising to continue with this approach. About a month later, Mr. W informed Hammond that "the plan of treatment was impossible" and therefore deserted any further attempts to accomplish Victorian sexual normalcy – a project in which he had invested a significant part of his life, energy, and capital.

Mr. W's perseverance concluded not only in acquiescence of his 'impossible' status, but also shortly after, in death. Hammond's last record of Mr. W noted that "he went into the civil war and was killed at either Antietam or Gettysburg."[37] Mr. W's disconformity may have prompted him to enlist in an effort perhaps to reclaim his masculinity, yet this is merely speculation. What was apparent throughout his life was his anguish in attempting to fulfill a fruitless pursuit of what had become classified as sexually 'normal.'

Misery loves the opposite
Of company, loneliness
Solitude in thought and practice
When that cyclical current churns out
Another lost fraction of a person
Who could have been:

Desireless Womanhood:
The Cases of Mrs. C and Mrs. O

Mrs. C was about twenty-five years old and had been married two years when she sought the assistance of Hammond. She professed upon arrival that she "loved her husband and was anxious to do all in her power to please him."[38] Women such as Mrs. C were framed as the guardians of domestic virtue, a gendered role that required an inexhaustible supply of spousal obedience and childcare service.[39] While the passionless or 'asexual Victorian woman' was upheld as an ideal for middle- to upper-class Euro-immigrant women in the period to maintain social respectability, sexual desire from both men and women was understood to be necessary in marriage.[40] A survey of Victorian women born prior to 1870 conducted by physician Clelia Mosher found that most women saw "the exchange of pleasure" in sexual intercourse to be a "worthy purpose in itself."[41] Contrary to the ideal of passionless womanhood, Victorian women and men alike "recognized and expressed sexual desire, interest, and passion" as "the *natural* physical accompaniment and distillation of romantic love" (emphasis added).[42] Although desirelessness suited the Victorian ideal of passionless womanhood, Mrs. C yearned not to embody this gendered ideal but to produce the sexual desires of most Victorian women for the purpose of better serving her husband.

Hammond's record of Mrs. C indicated that she conditioned herself to submit to the advances of her husband despite never having experienced "the slightest development of the sexual appetite, nor during her whole life had she experienced any feeling of desire."[43] Mrs. C's status as a married woman restricted her ability to assert agency and refuse submission. The state-controlled institution of marriage was already being condemned for such reasons in the period by prominent activists such as Victoria Woodhull, who declared in her 1871 speech in New York's Steinway Hall that "women must rise from their position as ministers to the passions of men to be their equals."[44]

Woodhull's critique of marriage was not an isolated incident in the period; in fact, "every word that Woodhull enunciated was familiar to moral reform, women's rights, Spiritualist, and free-love audiences."[45] Denunciation of marriage was an unquestionably reasonable stance for Victorian women to adopt, given the limited to non-existent agency women had to deny or otherwise refuse the sexual advances of their husbands, who were both socially and legally permitted to rape their wives. This differed from the life and law of the Haudenosaunee, where such acts were made unthinkable and women held much greater social influence and political power. Prominent early women's rights activists in the United States including Elizabeth Cady Stanton, Matilda Joslyn Gage, and Lucretia Mott were influenced by the Haudenosaunee in their own advocacy for women's autonomy from such ills as marital abuse and rape that were normalized in

Victorian America. Rape within marriage was not a prose-cutable offense in nineteenth-century case law, nor was the act of a husband sexually forcing themselves upon their wife defined as rape.[46] Hammond's record suggests that Mrs. C perceived her forced engagement in unwanted sexual encoun-ters to simply be an extension of her gendered duty to satisfy the sexual pleasures of her husband – a role that she believed she was failing to fulfill properly.

Hammond recorded that Mrs. C experienced emotional and physical distress as a wife and remarked that, although "sexual intercourse had never been painful to her," it had also never produced any pleasurable sensations, nor had she ever "experi-enced the orgasm." Even when "various devices had been tried with the object of developing sexual desire," Hammond noted that they only produced "a feeling of disgust" within her. While Mrs. C was subjected to repeated sexual contact despite being sex-repulsed, Hammond also referred to the case of Mrs. O, who had "never experienced sexual desire," but unlike Mrs. C held "no aversion to sexual intercourse" and derived "pleasurable sensations therefrom." Hammond reported that still "this did not excite desire for a repetition of the act; nei-ther did the caresses of her husband develop erotic feelings." He noted that this was despite the fact that Mrs. O's 'general health has always been excellent,' which evidently intrigued him.[47] Mrs. C and Mrs. O thus portray variances in their desire-lessness, with their differing responses toward engaging in sexual behavior. However, regardless of their respective repul-sion or indifference to sex, because both women occupied the gendered role of a Victorian wife, they were expected to stead-fastly submit to the sexual advances of their husbands as part of their pledge to marital duty.

The expectation of the wife to submit to the sexual

advances of the husband was "justified on medical grounds" as per sexological discourse, which claimed that "men would become seriously ill if their own sexual needs were not gratified" and that women could also experience "problems for her own reproductive system – so she would be doubly foolish to resist."[48] Although Mrs. C accepted this subjugation as part of her role as a wife, she yearned for alleviation from the unending expectations of Victorian womanhood, as recorded from Hammond's perspective: "I was obliged, however, to tell her that I thought her case to be out of the reach of medical science [. . .] I told her that it was barely possible that through the action of natural though unknown causes she might experience the relief she sought."[49]

As a guardian of Victorian cisheteropatriarchal norms, Hammond concluded that the possibility for relief could only exist on the condition that sexual desire be developed, which meant that Mrs. C's duty to pleasure her husband would take precedence over her relief. If Mr. W felt an impossible separation from marriage due to his inability to conform to masculine expectations, Mrs. C was wholly entrapped within marriage as a result of her feminine obligations.

Mrs. C was well aware that her desirelessness affected her ability to meet the expectations of Victorian womanhood. Hammond recorded that "she had always yielded willingly to the wishes of her husband, and was anxious to be, as she said, 'like other women.'"[50] Her remark "like other women" is the only directly quoted phrase provided by any of Hammond's patients. In a matrix of power that produced both 'normative' and 'non-normative' subjects, Mrs. C understood herself as the latter. Hammond's articulation of an "original absence of sexual desire" was seen as unnatural and incompatible with what sexology discourse had naturalized. Scholar Eunjung

Kim makes a parallel here with asexuality, observing that knowledge of asexuality is only made possible as it "is pathologized in the process of naturalizing sexual desire."[51]

Mrs. C's assessment of her predicament even prompted her to question whether she could become pregnant. Her apprehension may have been initiated by a lack of experiencing orgasm, since it was believed in the period that "a woman could not get pregnant if she failed to have an orgasm."[52] Despite her questioning, Hammond quelled Mrs. C's concerns and informed her that he "saw no reason why she might not become pregnant."[53]

Hammond based his assurance on his determination that Mrs. C's body was "well formed, and of healthy appearance." This indicates that pathologizing sexual desire as unnatural had opened Mrs. C's and other women's bodies up to intrusive physical inspection. He determined through examination that "the clitoris was found to be as well developed as it is in the majority of women; the ovaries could be distinctly felt, and were apparently normal, and the uterus was of full size," demonstrating the invasiveness of this procedure which classed her body as physically "normal."[54] Hammond made a similar conclusion regarding Mr. W's body, noting that he "undoubtedly [could] have mechanically gone through the act of intercourse."[55] Of another patient, labeled Mr. X, Hammond again stated that he "had never experienced sexual desire, though the organs were of full size and well-formed."[56] As the bodies of Hammond's patients appeared physically normative to him, he determined the cause of desirelessness to be a result of their internal sexual appetite being "underdeveloped."[57] Patients such as Mrs. C and Mr. W appeared externally "normal," yet were described as internally "defective."

Hammond indicated a few years after meeting with Mrs. C

that "she had a child, and her husband informed me that she was beginning to acquire sexual desire." He took the words of Mrs. C's husband as the truth, despite having no further contact with Mrs. C herself, and framed her to be much like what people today might consider a 'late bloomer:' "We see very frequently that certain mental characteristics make their appearance at a comparatively late period of life, and there is no reason, so far as I can perceive, why a like condition may not exist as regards the sexual appetite."[58] If we consider how Hammond framed desirelessness as a concealed defect that was open to emerge unpredictably, this could prompt us to also consider its power to escape diagnosis through not only its deviance from normative institutions, but also in its lack of perceptibility.

No you can't see me
And I tried to forget you
And sometimes I wonder
What would happen
If I stopped trying
So hard
To stop
Trying

(Un)civilized Desires

By the end of the nineteenth century, there was not only an understanding of a binary sex and binary gender system, but also a binary sexuality system composed of homosexuality and heterosexuality. Homosexuality was established by Victorian medical discourse as "neither normal nor natural."[59] Like other 'vices,' once identified, homosexuality was policed as a threat to civilization, especially as it became enmeshed with gender performance. This is when, according to Foucault, *the homosexual* became a species – "when it was transposed from the practice of sodomy onto a kind of interior androgyny, a hermaphrodism of the soul."[60] The establishment of a precise definition of homosexuality as an innate quality of a person regulated populations to avoid association with being labeled a homosexual and, by extension, dangerously 'unnatural.' Since association was then made on the basis of appearance or behavior, as upheld by medical discourse, this resulted in the strict policing of appearances and behaviors in the two-sexed world.[61] The 'heterosexual' and the 'homosexual' were forged in this way as mutually exclusive.

In contrast, sexual desirelessness maneuvered under the shroud of heterosexual normalcy in undetectable respects by its sheer inconceivability. Even when made evident by physicians such as Hammond, the congruence of desirelessness with the idealized claims of passionless womanhood and self-mastered masculinity also meant that it was interpreted as relatively non-threatening and even ideologically agreeable. Hammond himself spoke of desirelessness as a trait to be welcomed for the betterment of humanity, claiming that "women as a sex exhibit far less intensity of sexual desire than do men" and it would be "well for the future of the human race if a like retardation could be accomplished in males." Desirelessness was presented as Hammond's solution to the prevalence of vice and its connections to unrestrained male sexuality. Yet, rather than framing desirelessness as a natural development, Hammond upheld that it was "the education of women in civilized communities, and the restrictions imposed upon them by the customs of society" that "stand in the way of the development of the sexual appetite."[62]

External to *Sexual Impotence*, Hammond insisted that women were naturally inferior to men, claiming that their brains were "not suited to the work which required a man's brain" and were instead based in "emotion rather than intellect." He once stated that a woman was "not unlike a package of dynamite," and believed that women's sexuality was *naturally* volatile – an attitude in line with Victorian sexology discourse.[63] Women's bodies were discussed as inherently sexual, only being tamed by 'civilization' via the patriarchal institution of the family.[64]

While the subjugation of women's sexuality in the family was justified as necessary for the betterment of a 'civilized' society, men's sexual desire was not similarly pathologized or problematized. Despite Hammond's recognition of the problem of vice and his call for desirelessness to gain prevalence among men, men's sexual behavior was deemed permissible by Victorian society – at worst a 'problem' that could be dealt with through women's submission to men in marriage.

Like other either/or constructs, with the production and establishment of a 'civilized' norm, there was the generation of an antithesis, which Hammond and many others repeatedly referred to as the "savage." *Savage* was of course a racialized term that functioned as a marker for all peoples who were viewed as backward and brutish: the "races of Asia, Africa, and the Americas." Victorian anthropologists again used 'scientific' discourse to assert non-Europeanness as a marker of inferiority.[65] It's important to remember that sexology was not simply a gendered and sexual discourse, but a highly racialized one that reinforced the European superiority complex and provided a rationale for the ills of colonization.

Hammond utilized this coded rhetoric in his own constructions of sexual desire when referring to the role of vices in

stimulating sexual indulgence: "In *civilized* communities it will
always happen that such causes act with much greater force
than among *savages*, where, in fact, they are scarcely exhibited
at all, and where the promptings of nature are alone the incen-
tives to the act of copulation" (emphasis added).[66] He perceived
sexual desire to be malleable only within the varying constructs
that defined what he constituted as 'civilization,' while among
'savages' it functioned only as intended by 'primitive' nature.
Of course, Hammond believed that non-Europeans existed on
"a lower stage of evolutionary development."[67] These perceptions of mental inferiority embodied in the non-European and
non-male figure were enmeshed within Hammond's framing
of sexual desire, in which only a civilization dictated by European men could control the dangerous, naturally occurring
sexual desires of women and non-Europeans alike. As described
by scholar Ianna Hawkins Owen, the ideal of desirelessness was
utilized as a mechanism for justifying "racial domination of
whiteness over people of color and the not-quite-white."[68]
Hammond envisioned desirelessness to be incompatible with
'savages,' believing that the *natural* sexual drive would always
override their bodies.

Hammond's white supremacist perspective on sexual
desire was entwined with his religious outlook on morality
and the future of humanity being predicated on a sanctified
familial institution. In *Sexual Impotence*, he included a quote
by an unnamed English writer who claimed that "it is well for
the *sanctity* of the family" (emphasis added) that women lack
sexual desire.[69] Hammond also once stated that "there was no
morality in the world outside of the Christian religion."[70] His
perspective on the cisheteropatriarchal family as a holy institution framed unrestrained sexual desire as a threat to the
family and, by extension, civilization. Desirelessness was a

means to temper the dangers of excessive sexuality. What Hammond referred to as "original absence of sexual desire" took this to the furthest extreme. However, there was little indication that this concerned him, as demonstrated by his lack of urgency to devise a plan of treatment beyond self-persistence through sex.[71] This was unlike his plan of treatment for homosexuality, where he prescribed that homosexuals should regularly be burned or "cauterized [at] the nape of the neck and the lower dorsal and lumbar regions."[72]

However, by the turn of the century, an anxiety over the potential effects of desirelessness and other factors on lowering the reproduction rates of Euro-immigrant or white families was surfacing. Concerns emerged that, when "taken to an extreme, asexually-styled sensitivity and restraint could ultimately threaten white elite reproduction rates." As such, "a new marriage manual market pushed for the cultivation of erotic desire in monogamous, heterosexual marriage" away from Victorian ideals.[73] Falling rates of reproduction among Euro-immigrant or white middle-class women quickly propelled racist fears within eugenicists who "wanted only 'quality' families to increase."[74] These anxieties at the beginning of the twentieth century demonstrate how desirelessness posed a fundamental challenge to the state's attempt "to constitute a sexuality that is economically useful and politically conservative."[75] Desirelessness as an ideal thus disrupted the ability to ensure population control for the colonial state, since it could hypothetically reorient social norms away from reproducing the status quo.

This could provoke the question: How can bodies lacking sexual desire become productive machines of society? Those embodying desirelessness defied officialized discourses that upheld the belief of a naturalized sexual desire. However, the largely conformist actions of Hammond's patients provoked by intense social and medical regulation restricted any opportunity for them to find fulfillment outside of dominant expectations. Yet, this still inspires a further consideration regarding how embracing one's desirelessness can be a means of resisting the social expectations that constrict our lives by telling us we are broken. In other words, it can be a means of living as we are, escaping the chase of a social persona we are pressured into being everyday.

(Re)claiming Desirelessness

Without the ability to visibly mark them as abnormal, Hammond's patients eluded discernment in their desirelessness, indistinct and beyond explanation. Hammond was confounded by his inability to locate a perceptible cause for the condition of desirelessness among his patients, at one moment stating: "in this case there was nothing but original defect of organization[76] to which the lack of sexual desire could be attributed" and that because "we do not know in what part of the nervous system the sexual appetite is situated it is impossible to locate the abnormality."[77] The origins of desirelessness were unidentifiable by Hammond, meaning that any indication of its presence could only be gleaned through the confession of his patients.

While desirelessness could infiltrate and destabilize hegemonic social norms and binaries of gender, sex, and sexual desire, it has been made apparent that Hammond's patients largely compelled themselves to conformist approaches of navigating Victorian expectations. For Mr. W, it was the allure of a wife, a family, and the masculine-afforded privileges of embodying the Victorian ideal of normalcy. For

Mrs. C, and presumably Mrs. O, it was being conditioned to accept an objectified role of servicing the sexual advances of men through submission in marriage. The enduring desires of Hammond's patients to achieve normalcy were certainly not unique. Of a homosexual patient under Hammond's supervision, Henry Minton indicated the following:

> [Hammond] in 1883 declared a case of a man who was remorseful over engaging in anal homosexual relations and noted that his patient was "seriously desirous of being cured." [. . .] These private patients, however, struggling with their same-sex erotic feelings, may well have been searching for self-knowledge as much as treatment. Many were unaware of others like themselves, which may have motivated them to turn to medical practitioners [. . . in a] search for self-understanding.[78]

Minton's analysis suggests that patients whose sexuality was classified as 'abnormal' may not have merely been searching for correction by confessing their abnormalities to clinicians like Hammond, but relief through knowledge of their 'abnormality.' Mr. W and Mrs. C sought relief from the expectations of sexual desire, yet could not find a way to do so that brought them any feelings of contentment. However, there is a patient case recorded several years after Hammond's *Sexual Impotence* that reflected a different perspective.

Gardner Allen, a doctor from Boston, was receptive to Hammond's work and published an article in which he classified a man who was under his observation for about three years as reflecting Hammond's label of "original absence of all sexual desire." Allen described this patient as a 27-year-old brass-worker in excellent health who "never had any sexual feeling until the age of nineteen, when on climbing a post, he experienced a pleasurable sensation which suggested masturbation." After repeating this apparently gratifying act for about one week, the man claimed to have never repeated the act nor experienced any sexual feelings or desires again. Allen also recorded that the patient "never attempted coitus nor had any inclination to," adding that "the penis and testicles are apparently perfectly normal."

While Allen's discussion on his patient's normative anatomy or appearance was similar to that of Hammond and his patients, a critical divergence was evident in how Allen's patient perceived himself: "He seems utterly indifferent to his condition and entirely content to remain impotent."[79] Even in this man's probable isolation, Allen's patient was not concerned with conforming to the sexual expectations of Victorian manhood, but rather appeared content to be without sexual desire.

Allen's patient fundamentally deviated from sexuality's most essential principle of instituting a desire for sex in an age where a science of sexuality, at its apex, was claiming its place as undeniably natural through sexology discourse. Nonetheless, it would be disingenuous to ignore how the contented indifference of Allen's patient was tied to his male and presumably European status. From this place, he was afforded such entitlements to abstain from oppressive gendered and sexual expectations in a manner that was not similarly accessible to Victorian women (such as Mrs. O who was not reportedly sex-averse yet still subjected to the desires of her husband). Still, his representation as an individual who expressed contentment against the norms of sexual expectations and was able to remain untethered by them may inspire us to consider the question of our own relationship to desireless contentment.

Unhitched from the clutches of sexuality, Allen's patient exhibited how contentment in one's desirelessness could challenge the gendered norms and sexual expectations of Victorian America. His case reveals to us that to normalize fulfillment in our desirelessness can inspire the opening of portals to worlds unlike those which existed in an age of sexual desire; where men like Mr. W are no longer expected to be aggressively sexual, where women like Mrs. C can become detached from their submissive role as objects to the sexual advances of men, and where all social expectations tied to sexuality and gender can loosen and unravel, to be rearticulated anew.[80]

Open the floodgates to your soul
Let your dreams pour out like a river
Washing the pain of static away
Previously unimaginable you are always
Harboring the thoughts of ancients
Remember you are not all you
Got

On Love and the (A)romantic

There is a general social perception, in the West and Western-influenced world at least, that romantic relationships, in which mutual emotional and sexual attraction are present, are essential to a person's quality of life and general wellbeing.[1] Conversely, it is also commonly understood that a "failure to establish or maintain such relationships in general, and romantic relationships in particular, predicts both physical and emotional distress."[2] Studies have further attributed disengagement from romantic relationships with a decreased quality of life and an increased susceptibility to physical and mental health issues.[3] These assertions contour the lives of aromantic people, demarcating those of us who do not experience romantic attraction to be inherently closer to misery, sickness, and death.

Aros may internalize these narratives as we are repeatedly cast into the clutches of words like 'unfeeling,' 'robotic,' 'emotionless,' 'loveless,' and 'devoid' from a young age. From the outside looking in, aros can more easily identify which behaviors and expressions socially denote people as 'feeling' and, allegedly, more human than ourselves. Through my own 'outsider' eyes, romantic gestures sometimes seemed performative, as nothing more than simple reproductions of social scripts rooted in Western courtship practices, but to those who engaged in them they were imbued with meaning, to the extent that those who did not engage in them should be pitied and even pathologized.

Aros may come to feel as if their relationships or life will never be as fulfilling, or believe that they are 'unlovable' because of how essential romantic love is to the idea of living a healthy life. Since long-term relationships, in or out of marriage, carry the assumption that mutual romantic attraction is essential, aros can feel increasingly isolated when entering adulthood. And even though marriage is on the decline in the Western world, a 2014 Pew Research Study indicated that one-fifth of Americans over the age of twenty-five had never married, and that of those who had never married, about one-quarter were living with a partner,[4] while in Europe 71.2 per cent of families had a married couple at their center (as of 2015).[5] Although the social landscape is shifting and more people, especially within cities, are increasingly 'single,' romantic relationships are still upheld as a social expectation.[6]

Dominant discourses on what it means to be in love contour what is expected in a relationship and not only frame aro experiences, but apply to how we all communicate our affections, desires, and attractions. Even if we disagree or attempt to counter the hegemony of these discourses, we risk the ostracization and backlash that come with defiance or difference from their standards. It only makes sense then that we give these notions of love and romance more scrutiny so that we may deconstruct how they are connected to the idea of living a 'healthy' or 'fulfilling' life.

Love Hierarchies

What many of us may see as *love* in relationships today is largely defined through the lens of romance. The notion of *romantic love* is "a highly specific cultural complex, one that originated in Western Europe in the eighteenth century,"[7] and was exported throughout the world via colonial apparatuses. However, romantic love has not always held such a grip over relationship formation. Whereas marriage had primarily been organized through families as a tool for arranging economic affairs prior to the mid-eighteenth century, the rise of the notion of romantic love reoriented this practice. A 2017 article for the National Women's History Museum in the United States summarized this transitional moment:

> As expectations increased that marriage would be built on a foundation of love rather than mutual economic interest, the way that partners were selected had to evolve. When parents stopped making the selection, prospective lovers needed to find one another and then determine the extent of mutual attraction. Courtship became a distinctive phase of partner selection, and familiar rituals evolved.[8]

This is not to say that what could be referred to as 'romance' did not exist prior to this historical moment, just that the emergence of romantic discourses worked to reorient social norms and practices of mass populations.[9]

Romanticism, or the Romantic movement, gained social traction in the West in the eighteenth century and cast *passionate love* into a positive light. This shift in mainstream attitudes in favor of romantic love has been attributed to the rise of the novel, which played the social role of "preaching 'the gospel' of romantic love to a generation of largely middle-class young women."[10] Eliza Haywood's novel *Love in Excess* (1719–20) reflected the "cultural shift toward a companionate model of marriage" while challenging social expectations that inhibited expressions of women's sexual desire.[11] In early eighteenth-century England, popular narratives such as these made the novel synonymous with "a short story of romantic love."[12] The social role that the novel played continues to be filled today by cinema and television, which perpetuate romantic ideals of what it means to be 'in love' among the mass public.[13]

Romantic love gradually became regarded as the primary reason to select a life partner, and this social change was initially received with much contention.[14] Concerns emerged over romantic's love potential to encourage the deification of lovers when "bound to the service of the individual human ego and its desire for power."[15] Mary Shelley addressed this in her novel *Valperga* (1823) when she noted the inclination of the subject in love to "idolize the object; and, placing him apart and selecting him from his fellows, look at him as superior in nature to all others." She furthermore argued:

> If we separate him [the idolized love object] from his fellow mortals, so do we separate ourselves, and, glorying in belonging to him alone, feel lifted above all other sensations, all other joys and griefs, to one hallowed circle from which all but his idea is banished; we walk as if a mist or some more potent charm divided us from all but him; a sanctioned victim which none but the priest set apart for that office could touch and not pollute, enshrined in a cloud of glory, made glorious through beauties not our own.[16]

Shelley saw romantic love as a danger that could result in "a delusive effort at deification of self and beloved that ends with the victimization and sacrifice of the woman on the altar of passion," as noted by Kari Lokke.[17] Skepticism toward romantic or passionate love was deeply rooted in the Western philosophical tradition since, prior to the Romantic movement, it was predominantly interpreted in the West as a dangerous force that could lead to delusion, such as it was framed in classical, medieval, and neo-classical thought.[18] Plato, for instance, spoke of a man's passion or "love to procreate" as being rooted in *irrationality* – "a form of madness in which a man loses his mind – or more literally, his brain."[19]

Plato and other Ancient Greek figures, who would become canonical in the history of Western 'civilization,' inferiorized passionate love between men and women in favor of a different formation of love that would come to be termed, many years after the decline of Ancient Greek life, *platonic* love. Plato's writings and Ancient Greek philosophy were carried forward by numerous European scholars through a movement known as neoplatonism. This included scholars such as Marsilio Ficino, who, in the fifteenth century, translated Plato's works into Latin and subsequently coined the term *amor platonicus*, or platonic love.[20] Ficino used the term synonymously with *amor socraticus* to reference affection between an older man and a younger man, such as between Socrates and his pupils.[21]

By the 1630s, the meaning of the term *platonic love* began to be associated with 'nonsexual love' between men and women, where it was characterized in English stage plays as a pretentious and unattainable ideal.[22] In William Davenant's *The Platonick Lovers* (1636), the playwright "mocks the idea of Platonic love by contrasting the love of two characters, Theander and Eurithea, as impossibly lofty in contrast to the more carnal-oriented desires of Phylomont and Ariola."[23]

Throughout the eighteenth and nineteenth centuries, the idea of platonic love continued to be framed in this manner in literary works, "often with the underlying suggestion that love separated from sexual desire was an absurd pretense."[24] In *Pamela; or, Virtue Rewarded* (1740), a popular English epistolary novel written with the expressed intent "to cultivate the principles of virtue and religion in the minds of youth of both sexes," author Samuel Richardson wrote through the character's point of view: "I am convinced, and always was, that *platonic love* is *platonic nonsense*: the persons pretending to it may, where the best is meant, be compared to the fly buzzing about the blaze, till its wings are scorch'd." Through this character, Richardson argued that platonic love could and should only be found in old age, and raised concerns over its presence among young people.[25]

Other authors similarly framed platonic love as socially threatening. In *A Warning to Wives: Or The Platonic Lover: A Novel* (1848), Harriette Smythies explained her views on platonic love through the dialogue of two characters. In her story, Fitzopal, a character who believes in the possibility of platonic love, is accused of seducing his friend's wife by his uncle, Grumbleby. In response, Fitzopal asserts that his love is *only* platonic and argues that he is "capable of that refined, exalted, and delicate sentiment called Platonic Love – something more tender than friendship, less mundane than passion!" In response, Grumbleby asserts that "there is no such thing as Platonic Love between a man and a woman" and professes to Fitzopal: "Don't deceive yourself – don't deceive her! [. . .] Give up this most dangerous intimacy."[26] Novels such as these served as powerful advice-literature to shape attitudes of how attraction *should* function 'normally' in relationships.

In academic works of this period, the concept of platonic love was equally viewed with skepticism. In *A Lecture on Love* (1816), the unnamed author recorded how the idea of platonic relationships was often "censured as dangerous and ridiculed as absurd." They hypothesized that "if such there be [Platonic love] on Earth, the sexual feeling must be purely mental," and thus attributed the presence of *nonsexual love* to a transference of sexual desire from body to mind.[27] Even though the concept of platonic love was evidently mocked and distrusted, its presence in the social imagination still initiated a discourse on a form of love that was independent from sexual desire, even if many adopted the angle that it was only possible in limited contexts or in theory. This discourse stands as a testament to how the idea that love could exist independently from sex has been commonly discredited as 'impossible' in the West for hundreds of years. Even so, this conversation surrounding platonic love that pervaded the ideological landscape of Europe itself strayed from what Plato himself believed.

Henry T. Finck wrote in *Romantic Love and Personal Beauty* (1887) that platonic love was commonly understood among the public as "a friendship between a man and a woman from which all traces of passion are excluded."[28] However, Finck himself disagreed with this definition on the basis that it was "utterly foreign to Plato's way of thinking," stating that "platonic love has nothing to do with women whatever" and rather should refer to "an attachment between a man and a youth."[29] Finck stated that the most apparent example of platonic love could be seen in Plato's *Symposium* between Alcibiades and Socrates. It is here that Plato recorded the

'Speech of Alcibiades,' in which the Greek statesman professed his deep affections for Socrates:[30]

> Whenever I listen to him, my frenzy is greater than that of
> the Corybantes. My heart pounds and tears flood out when
> he speaks, and I see that many people are affected in the same
> way. [. . .] Even now I'm well aware that if I allowed myself
> to listen to him I couldn't resist but have the same experience
> again. He makes me admit that, in spite of my great defects, I
> neglect myself and instead get involved in Athenian politics.
> So I force myself to block my ears and go away, like someone
> escaping from the Sirens, to prevent myself sitting there
> beside him till I grow old.[31]

This example of platonic love taken directly from *Symposium*
illustrated a relationship that, as Finck characterized, "should
be formed between a man and a youth, not too young, but
when his beard begins to grow and his intellect to develop"
that lasts a lifetime.[32] When translated in modern terminology, Finck wrote that this type of relationship resembled
"the language of modern Romantic Love," except between
two males rather than a man and a woman.[33]

This type of relationship among males was what Marsilio
Ficino referenced in Plato's writings when he coined the term
amor platonicus in the fifteenth century. However, over time,
"as Ficino's description of Platonic love circulated around
Europe, women stepped into the role of the beloved who
incites spiritual desire," wrote Juliet Lapidos in an article for
Slate.[34] For Finck, this alteration in definition troubled him
deeply, stating on the subject of platonic love in 1887 that "the
most incorrect and absurd notions universally pervade
modern literature and conversation."[35] Finck disagreed with

the notion that platonic love could be used to refer to relationships involving women on the grounds of, what he referenced as, Plato's own "contempt for women."[36] To substantiate his claim, Finck cited *Timaeus*, in which Plato wrote:

> [. . .] all those creatures generated as men who proved themselves cowardly and spent their lives in wrong-doing were transformed,[37] at their second incarnation, into women. And it was for this reason that the gods at that time contrived the love of sexual intercourse by constructing an animate creature of one kind in us men, and of another kind in women.[38]

For Plato, non-human lifeforms were also reincarnations of male deficiency that were organized in a hierarchy. He claimed that "the tribe of birds are derived by transformation, growing feathers in place of hair, from men who are harmless but light-minded,"[39] while those "which lives in the water, came from the most utterly thoughtless and stupid of men, whom those that remolded them deemed no longer worthy even of pure respiration."[40] Thus, for Plato, women were just another step in this hierarchy under the more 'perfect' man. This was exhibited as well in *Laws*, Plato's last work, which was left unfinished at the time of his death (346 BCE). In Book 6, he wrote that "females are inferior in goodness to males" and that "women would not so much as listen to the mention of the right rule without shrieks of indignation."[41]

On this basis, Finck described how platonic love between males was upheld as superior to romantic or passionate love between men and women in Ancient Greek society. He argued that, in general, the latter was seen as inferior on account of its dependency on the body, while the former was interpreted as superior on account of its association to the soul. As Finck referred to it, platonic love was defined by "a passionate, romantic friendship between men and boys, which (whether it really existed or not) the pupils of Socrates dilate upon as the only noble, exalted form of passion that is presided over by Eros."[42] In *Symposium*, the allegedly higher form of love, or platonic love between males, is one in which the pursuit of sexual gratification and "the physical dimension of love is wholly absent and the lover is positively motivated [only] to promote the boyfriend's virtue." In contrast, the more *common love* was perceived as a love that was "purely physical" and, when directed toward women, "taken to be non-rational."[43] While in the Ancient Greek context platonic love was regarded as the superior form of love, this was conversely the case for Finck, whose agenda for discussing platonic love was in using it as an example of how romantic love reflected the more 'civilized' nature of nineteenth-century Western Victorian society in contrast to the 'primitive' and non-European world.

Finck outlined a love hierarchy in the introduction of *Primitive Love and Love-stories* (1899):

> [. . .] there is a large number of sentimental writers who make the extraordinary claim that the lower races, however savage they may be in everything else, are like ourselves in their amorous relations; that they love and admire personal beauty as we do. The main object of the present volume is to demolish this doctrine; to prove that sexual refinement and the sense of personal beauty are not the earliest but the latest products of civilization.[44]

This love hierarchy is encoded in the terms Finck used, defining romantic love as "an ecstatic adoration of a woman by a man or of a man by a woman."[45] Here, Finck's *adoration of women* contrasted with a *contempt for women*, the latter of which he credited to "the lower races in all parts of the world"[46] as well as authors of antiquity, such as Plato, who looked upon women as "inferior beings."[47]

The phrase *contempt for women* was frequently used in the period to characterize non-European peoples as generally inferior to the colonizing European culture – the obvious reason being to justify European colonization; to frame it as a necessary 'civilizing mission.' An 1845 article in the *Calcutta Review* argued that "all natives, even the best educated among them, have a profound contempt for women and regard them as formed alone for their pleasure."[48] Similarly, an 1828 book by J. C. Beltrami about the Indigenous peoples of Turtle Island argued that "it is unquestionably this contempt for women which retards civilization and increases the ferocity of these unfortunate tribes."[49] In line with this trend, Finck himself attributed a contempt for women as "the attitude of Africans, Australians, Polynesians, Americans, and others."[50] Conversely, he framed the romantic "adoration of women, individually or collectively, [as] an entirely modern phenomenon, and is even now very far from universal."[51] Of course, Finck spoke of himself as a modern romantic man – an inherent result of Western *advancement* – and claimed to have "worshipped" women.[52]

The social prioritization of platonic love as a relationship between males was thus framed by Finck as an illustration of Greek contempt for women, and, as a result, meant that the Greeks too could not be considered a fully civilized race.[53] This reflected dominant Western attitudes of the time, as Greeks in the nineteenth and early twentieth centuries were seen as inferior to Western Europeans and 'Anglo-Saxons' and therefore not welcome under the umbrella of whiteness.[54] For Finck, Plato's Greekness was thus not a mere descriptor of his identity, but inherent to what Finck alleged to be the more universally Greek "contempt for women." As Finck wrote, "In thus excluding women from the sphere of pure, super-sensual romantic love, Plato shows himself a Greek to the marrow."[55] Nevertheless, for Finck and others, the Greeks were still regarded as more civilized than the 'less refined' and less European 'lower races' in the colonial love hierarchy:

> The Greeks, instead of confuting my theory that romantic love is the last product of civilization, afford the most striking confirmation of it. While considering the love-affairs of Africans, Australians, and other uncivilized peoples, we were dealing with races whose lack of intelligence and delicacy in general made it natural to expect that their love, too, must be wanting in psychic qualities and refinement. But the Greeks were of a different calibre. Not only their men of affairs – generals and statesmen – but their men of thought and feeling – philosophers and poets – were among the greatest the world has ever seen; yet these philosophers and poets, who, as everywhere, *must have been far above the emotional level of their countrymen in general* – knew nothing of romantic love.[56]

While Finck initially wrote of this as a rather peculiar phenomenon, he eventually suggested that a link between Athens and Asia could be to blame: "Indeed, when we examine Greek life in the light of comparative *Culturgeschichte*,[57] we find a surprising prevalence of Oriental customs and ideas, especially in Athens, and particularly in the treatment of women."[58]

He characterized the Japanese similarly in terms of being simultaneously 'civilized' yet 'backward,' stating that "Japanese civilization is in many important respects far superior to ours; yet in their treatment of women and estimate of love, this race has not yet risen above the barbarous stage." With this assertion in mind, Finck concluded that "we should have to deny them the epithet of the civilized."[59]

This love hierarchy was thus invested in using *romantic love*, or a claimed adoration of women by men, as an indicator of Western advancement and white supremacy. Love was therefore used as a colonial instrument to justify the European superiority complex, enshrining narratives of the 'backward' primitive dark past and the enlightened romantic white future into the greater social imagination as 'truth,' while suffocating the agency of so-called primitive women under a blanket of paternalism and saviorism.

Many of the arguments that Finck relied on to situate and substantiate his claims were, of course, skewed through the lenses of Western anthropologists, sociologists, and scientists, whose reports carried officialized status throughout the colonial world. For example, Finck cited Euro-immigrant anthropologist Lewis H. Morgan among other alleged "competent observers" to express that the Indigenous peoples of Turtle Island and Abya Yala were devoid of love.[60] Morgan wrote in *Systems of Consanguinity and Affinity of the Human Family* (1871) that "in his native state, the Indian is below the passion of love. It is entirely unknown among them."[61] Similarly, prominent English politician and scientist John Lubbock wrote in *The Origin of Civilisation and the Primitive Condition of Man* (1870) that among "savages" and the "lowest races," the notion of "true love is almost unknown to them; and marriage, in its lowest phases, is by no means a matter of affection and companionship."[62]

Sanctioned off from the allegedly greater and more spiritual *romantic love*, the only love that "lower races" were deemed capable of in this hierarchy was *sensual* – of and relating purely to the body; which was seen as a synonym for *irrational*,

brutish, or *barbarous*, and thus *uncivilized behavior*.[63] This officialized discourse espoused by Finck and others, "who
maintained that [so-called] primitive people were incapable
of love,"[64] fueled social attitudes that propelled the violent
trajectory of the larger colonial project forward. In the colonial (il)logic, committing genocide and land theft against
an allegedly *inferior*, *irrational*, and *loveless* people somehow
seemed to make it all more acceptable.

This notion of who was deemed capable of 'true love,'
which was equated to romantic love, thus regulated who was
considered more worthy of life and who was more 'justifiably'
subject to genocide, slavery, mass incarceration, and policing.
Scholar Paulette Richards described how slaveholders portrayed enslaved Africans as irrational and "incapable of love" and
"propagated these myths as a rationalization for the practice of
breaking up families on the auction block." She notes how stereotypes that portrayed Black women as sensual "lascivious
jezebels who seduced white men" were conjured to rationalize
their sexual abuse.[65] These narratives and practices supporting
chattel slavery persist in our colonial present to continue to
enforce the policing and mass incarceration of Black people.

Clevis Headley reflects on how Black men are socially
framed in the modern colonial world as "naturally unethical"
and therefore as "incapable of love," writing that "those who
are naturally predisposed to harming others are incapable of
love, because they lack the emotional capacity to empathize
with others." This stereotype has situated Black men as inherently criminal and thus 'justifiably' under the control and
regulation of policing and mass incarceration. This colonial
narrative of Black men as *loveless*, or without the capacity to
experience 'true' or 'romantic' love, is exemplified in "the
insistent association of Black males with a hypersexuality

savagely expressed in sexual violation and exploitation" that reduces Black men "to their sexual organs."[66] While Black men are framed as driven by "untamed animal urges," white men are regarded in the dominant social narrative as being "more or less able to think clearly and rationally."[67] In officialized discourses shielded and projected by the facade and power of modern colonial institutions, whiteness reflects the rational, spiritual, and romantic, more deserving of love and life, while Blackness represents the more bodily, sexual, and loveless, and thus more deserving of disdain and death.

While these colonial narratives and practices of lovelessness and hierarchy are not 'all-powerful,' meaning that we have agency not to abide by them and even to collectively deconstruct them, they can quickly and damagingly become internalized, especially in environments and contexts in which they are upheld and where critiques of them remain absent. This is often the case for communities who may be conceptualized as 'colonized.' For example, Adaljiza Sosa Riddell noted how "Chicanos have had and continue to have, very little control over their self-image, cultural awareness, and self-definition" in the modern colonial world.[68] This lack of control over one's self-image is rooted in colonial power dynamics in which official narratives of 'history' and 'truth' have been told to us through the eyes and minds of the colonizers for hundreds of years.[69] Living in a settler colony, colonized people are often conditioned "to internalize negative images of themselves and their culture" while being conditioned to "seek Anglo approval for their actions." This can manifest a dynamic in which "the colonized adopts the world view of the colonizer and may even become a suboppressor of his own people." This is a form of psychic colonial violence that fulfills itself when stereotypes are "internalized and articulated as positive cultural attributes by the group in question" and then become perceived as inherent.[70] Thus, without critique, internalization can end up not only reproducing colonial narratives and practices, but result in them being celebrated as if they are essential parts of ourselves and our communities.

To end the pursuit of what has been parroted as truth for hundreds of years and has shaped our physical world is thus a difficult task. It leads us to ask, given the hierarchical ways in which love has been used as a device by the colonial machine, how can we *decolonize* love?

The love machine spins my gears
Alters codes in my brain
Flips the switch on/off
Loner on the road to nowhere
Out of love, but still
Intuition lights the stars
On fire, shows me otherwise
Worlds, the universe
Are nothing but

Unsettling the Romantic Order

In a globalized world deeply shaped by Western colonialism and cultural imperialism, the idea of romantic love has reached almost every region of human settlement on Earth. Where romantic currents are weaker, romance may be understood as less important or not necessary to relationship formation and marriage.[71] In these non-romantic or 'less romantic' contexts, partners in a relationship may engage in behaviors and describe their love for one another in terms that might appear totally unloving or loveless to people encultured by the romantic West. When relationship formation on the basis of factors other than romantic love occurs, Western romantics will commonly interpret these relationships as backward or as a legacy of an immoral practice – one that the 'civilizing mission' failed to eradicate. The romantic outlook still generates inferiorizing narratives deeply attached to notions of what it means to be 'civilized,' just as it did historically.

Romantic love still forms an essential part of the socially expected individualistic life trajectory that requires attracting a suitor and forming a 'productive' marriage. Romantic love has thus come to function "as the bait, so to speak, for marriage, helping young people to cut ties from their childhood home" and engage in this pursuit.[72] From marriage, there is the expectation that a family unit will form and establish themselves in their own private home, usually, although not always, distant from networks and without support systems of extended family and community. This is promoted throughout Western institutional apparatuses, whether medical, political, or educational, and naturalized as if it were essential to living a 'normal' and 'productive' life, despite its tendencies to alienate.[73] This is because, as phrased by Conrad Kanagy and Donald Kraybill, "producing and selling romantic love has become big business in societies that need romance to serve as the foundation of nuclear families."[74]

Failure to pursue and actualize this is construed as a failure on the part of the individual – a reflection of their defective, pitiful, repulsive, or unlovable nature. Under capitalist cisheteropatriarchy, this perception becomes most imposed onto single women. As mentioned, there is a historical pattern here. While Henry Finck professed that romantic love allegedly reflects an *adoration of women*, in *Romantic Love and Personal Beauty* (1887) he also noted that "men, so to speak, pitch upon the girls they can see: those who are completely negative, unnoticeable, colourless, formless, invisible, are left behind." It is thus on the woman to make her character distinguishable or her "*individuality* felt" by a man.[75]

Because, under capitalist cisheteropatriarchy, women have been largely dependent on relationship formation with men for economic stability, to cater to a man's individualistic sensibilities, especially those of white men, became an essential part of everyday survival in the modern colonial world. The presence of this gendered and racialized dynamic has only shifted slightly as some women have gained marginally more economic independence and have pushed back against social stigmas surrounding single-womanhood.[76] However, the idea that men should be equal to women in this romantic relational dynamic still produces fanfare and strong misogynist currents directed toward women who challenge colonial cisheteropatriarchy.

Mary Shelley's concerns over romantic love's tendency to alienate us through a "deification of self and beloved that ends with the victimization and sacrifice of the woman on the altar of passion," expressed in the early nineteenth century, remain relevant today.[77] Yet, part of the reason why romance remains so idolized is because of the way it romanticizes individual choice "driven by personal feelings and emotions" as the greatest exemplification of 'freedom' attainable on Earth – paralleling capitalist desires of individual choice in consumption practices, 'private property,' and elsewhere.[78] Because the presence of romantic love is viewed as a reflection of freedom in the West, it has become interpreted as the only way to love freely.[79] It keeps us in pursuit or, as Kari Lokke mentioned, "bound to the service of the individual human ego and its desire for power."[80] Thus, even when romance fails to hold relationships together, the pursuit of romantic love is often not credited as the cause for such failure, which is rather attributed to the incompatibility of individual partners.

In the wake of the Romantic movement, romance was understood as an experience in which an individual falls under "the spell of aesthetic beauty and find[s] life reflecting some striking artistic ideal or instance." Romance continues to carry, in almost all cases, "an aesthetic connotation; it often indicates a captivating form or a show of passion," so much so that it "implicitly unites love and art."[81] Romantic love is therefore entwined with the capacity for an individual to make aesthetic judgment, which itself was historically ordered through the language of race to be attainable *only* by a particular 'rational' subject or Man, as described by Rizvana Bradley and Denise Ferreira da Silva:

> The Subject's *sensus communis*, of course, only emerges through the constitutive excommunication of the Savage (THE CONQUERED), the Negro (THE COMMODITY), the Primitive (THE OTHER), and the Traditional (THE UNDERDEVELOPED) – figures who nevertheless come to haunt Man as the bearers of an ontological dissonance, an immanent declension, we might call blackness.[82]

Who was deemed capable of making aesthetic judgment directly correlates with who was deemed capable of romantic love. We can again see how this worldview came to inspire and uphold narratives that the non-European was incapable of love and feeling. Why then should inclusion into this worldview built on explicit *excommunication* be pursued at all?

Is it a coincidence that identities like *aromantic*, *asexual*, and *agender* have emerged and been largely encircled by the European (and Euro-immigrant) subject? Is their creation dependent on this subject's expression of one's divergence from norms that were constructed with the *exclusive* inclusion of the European subject within them? Is identity formation in this context not a move to dismantle or refuse, but rather a precise move to legitimate oneself within the structure via the categorical identity that becomes attached as a 'part' to the very notion of the self? What does it mean for the non-subject (non-European), who was always already situated as external to Western constructs of romance, sexuality, and gender, to claim an identity that reflects that very external-ity? Is it redundant (yet, at the same time, does it reinforce the structure's legitimacy)? What might happen when we reori-ent our discourses of love, sex, and gender through the actualization of a way of being in the world that is uncoupled from the 'rational' complex of aesthetic judgment?

The latter question is not a pursuit of a 'new' kind of exist-ence, but rather an acceptance that this is the state of being that always already finds itself anywhere and everywhere. In other words, even if aesthetic judgment and the 'rational' romantic order claim authority over life – the universe – it does not *actu-ally* make it so. To attempt to designate the 'laws' of the universe is as preposterous as it is destructive to all of us caught in the wake of this 'God complex.' I recall how the symbolism of the flagpole, stuck into the Earth as a signification of Man's claim to 'ownership,' snaps like a twig the moment the universe has aligned it to be so in a form of wordless poetry.

Unsettling the romantic order invites us to reorient the terms through which romanticism has been assigned and assigns value. It allows us to understand 'beauty' not in purely

individualized aesthetic terms, but in what is collectively beneficial for all living things. Thus, this romantic unsettling may
encourage us to love things about ourselves differently, love
things about our relationality differently, and love things about
life differently. Hortense Spillers spoke to how this reorientation of value away from the romantic sense may be reflected:

> So what you love in the other person is not the way they look,
> you love their courage, or their character, or their power to
> resist, or their being strong in the face of danger, or perhaps
> even stepping overboard or over the line of danger. Then love
> is predicated on something other than our romantic sense.[83]

As resistance to the colonial capitalist matrix remains ongoing,
this reorientation of value disturbs the aesthetic-oriented narratives of romance across space-time. This is a love that does
not ignore oppression by devoting itself only to aesthetic hierarchies or displays of 'beauty,' in which considerations to
colonial power dynamics are absent, or taken with little regard.
It rejects the romanticization of oppressive figures in society –
the enforcers, the 'wealthy,' the directors.

While symbols of 'success' in the modern colonial world go
hand-in-hand with those who are romanticized as beautiful or
attractive, a love that is *decolonial* is built on interconnectivity
and builds community. Colonialism, as a force of institutionalized lovelessness, has sought to control, destroy, and regulate
the presence of love, especially among Indigenous and 'colonized' peoples. There are all types of institutions and control
complexes in the modern colonial world where love is made
to be *difficult*: a liability, a risk, a weight on one's own individualized 'success' and survival.

In these everyday *loveless* contexts, love outside of its

romantic context has been made to become so unfamiliar that its presence in communities has become viewed with skepticism, distrust, and mockery. Love is attacked and suppressed by the romantic or 'ordered world' because it is a threat. What else could explain the targeted violence of people who love all their relations, human and more-than-human,[84] enough to protect them? It is from under these intense conditions of institutionalized lovelessness that a concept like *decolonial love* even becomes necessary to distinguish from romantic love, as there is an everyday urgency to refuse how love has been framed by so-called rational aesthetic judgment; for us to break through the illusions and remember what love is, not what it has been made to be.

What we might call decolonial love today long pre-dates romantic love. While romantic love focuses on the pursuit of individual fulfillment through relationship formation, decolonial love destabilizes the primacy of individual freedom above all else,[85] instead being based in communal strength and interdependency through relational networks of love and support. The phrase *decolonial love* was first mentioned in Chicana feminist Chela Sandoval's book *Methodology of the Oppressed* (2000), where she destabilized "the narrative of love as encoded in the West."[86] Sandoval spoke of love not in romantic terms, but as "a body of knowledges, arts, practices, and procedures for re-forming the self and the world."[87] This is a love that is framed in opposition to the violence, hatred (including self-hatred), and death perpetuated by the colonial matrix of power. Rather than focusing on love as defined in romantic terms, this is a love that "begins from within, and from below or through the subjectivities of communities who have risen and resisted colonial forces, as they pursue modes of healing and liberation."[88] To decolonize love then is to deconstruct the hierarchies that have been made in its name and to understand its power as the foundation of a community-building movement toward liberation.[89] It is to imagine and develop ethical relationships that work toward achieving "a radical repair/reparation in the modern/colonial world."[90]

Rather than an emphasis on our individualism then, decolonial love refocuses our attention on our relationality. In *Spiral to the Stars: Mvskoke Tools of Futurity* (2019), Laura Harjo elaborated:

> [. . .] a praxis of decolonial love is based foremost on love for community, which is distinct from a heterosexual notion of romantic love. To love community is to work in service to one's community. There is a dimension of responsibility – that is, an intention of concern – and a dimension of care: that is, the act of tending to community. [. . .] Hence, decolonial love structures the resurgence and amplification of community's spiritual and relational power.[91]

Tending to kinship networks as a person marked as a *queer* in the modern colonial world is a journey rife with pain, transformation, and navigating cycles of violence. Since we are often excluded from our communities because of how colonial structures have demonized our queerness, decolonial love calls for us to do what might seem 'impossible'; asking us to love ourselves so that we become strong enough, more assured of our interconnections and our interiority, to love our communities; urging us to make life meaningful beyond the pursuit to fulfill the expectation of individualized romantic relationship formation.

Unclouded by romantic pursuits, aromanticism can open

space for us to actualize decolonial love in our lives.[92] Coming into our aromanticism is, in essence, an ending of a pursuit, as we pull away from romance's hold over our life trajectories and come to make meaning of our lives differently. It is in this place where a concept like decolonial love can take precedence over romantic love. This is reflected in the poem 'Care, uncoupled' published on *AZE* by UnYoung, who urges the reader to imagine mutual care or love for one another external to any romantic implications. As UnYoung writes, this is a vision made possible through the action of *uncoupling*, that is, untangling the association between intimacy and care from romance and desirability.[93] Through such an aromantic perspective, a concept like decolonial love becomes more clear. When we are not caught in a pursuit of romance, we may be more apt to dream and act beyond its borders – to recognize and respect love as a force of community unification and liberation.

Aromantic Love Poems

In the following series of poems, I reflect on the notion of love through an aromantic and decolonial lens. These are my love poems, my notes on love expressed through the poetic voice.

I
Love isn't easy
It sticks to my bones
Reveals itself in the bags under my eyes
Dissolves the clouds hanging over my hopes for a better world

It comforts me
As I torture my body, contemplating
It holds my hand, keeps me from crumbling
Like the sticky glue on an elementary school science project

Love is the battery
Destabilizes center of gravity
Hovers me over vacant space
Tucks my eyelids under the sky

It lulls me to sleep
Carves caverns into my hardened walls
Falls in a demanding silence
Like the dinner table of a dysfunctional family

It cannot be reduced
To the blurred or tainted imagination
Left underneath shadows hidden
Or trapped by any dogma that masquerades as its captor

Love remains uncontained
When I am no longer in this body
All drawn out
And spread across the universe

2
Told to be cold
So I covered myself in ice
Rested my eyes on needles
Strangled my moving body

For the appreciation of others
To not be myself
Was told was better
For everyone else

3

When does the ship stop sailing towards 'perfection'
Or hopeless homogeneity
Tell me, when do things get interesting for people like you
    and me?

4

Hurt me
Hurt me more
For my love
Is out the door

And so are you . . .

5

My desire is caught in a balancing act of rising peril
How much is my own, how much is my response to
    conditions beyond my control
But control is an illusion anyway and so is the game of life
The ways we say this is wrong and this is right
Propels me back to the highwire, switching masks for the
    crowd below

6

Aromanticism is a declaration
Of disinterest in being captured in relics
Of a time long passing

Before my mind's eye the windows flash
Like portals into dimensions that see love differently

7

Sometimes it *feels* like I am suspended
In vacancy, floating but not free
A body held through spirit
Magnetically

Sometimes it *feels* like all is not lost
Like we can rearrange fluidity
Fall through the cracks in space
Take new shape

Sometimes it *feels* like the beautiful
Is all one thing, with many permutations
And love, how we do it
Is just one

8

But what can I say as a 'colonized' 'aromantic'
You may say the ancestral is 'lost'
But I am here
Picking up the pieces
Of what's been made to be
My present, refusing to drown
Knowing that we have learned to speak in 'new' tongues
To translate the 'old'
And what is that process
But love

9

More and more I feel
It is okay to be 'alone'
Without

Filled with doubt
Sometimes I tire of the games
We play

But I grow more assured
As I traverse the cliff's edge
Surrounded

By some different future
Not yet realized I thrust myself
Into blank space

10

What if I told you that we could learn to love magic
Undiscover comfort in the unknown
Deconstruct desirability and leave the pursuit
Rotting on the table, unfit for our consumption

Would the smell of its decaying flesh
Remind you of something?
Would it awaken
Everything inside of you?

11

'Why doesn't [insert name] have a girlfriend slash
    boyfriend yet?'
My eyes want to roll back down the mountain I climbed
    up from to be here
But I stare forward blankly

One day I'll learn to laugh
When it all blows up
In my face

That those who police are prisoners
Trapped in their pursuit of 'order'
In a universe ruled by chaos

With my head in the clouds I am closer
To making everything I digest
Irrelevant

Closer to riding the skyline
And returning to the edge
Of the universe

I guess then prompts my response:
Are you really ready
to know?

12

Not so long ago
The missionaries came
Believed they were destiny manifesting
By official statements

Recorded as accurate
On actions embedded in the land
The 'burden' to 'civilize'
Some say they acted *out* of love
Benev(i)olence
Yes, they did
outside of it, yes
Because their disrespect to life
Speaks louder

13

Walking on weathered path
Between hills and the rocky
Rolling air howling
Around me, she
Tears through the barrier
Lifts me up the mountain
Makes me remember
What it means to be *in* love

14

Maybe

  the thing I am

    is stuck

      trying to tell myself

       that I (do not) need

        anyone else

         to make me feel

          complete

15

A romantic for a better world
A romantic the driver
A romantic keeps me awake
A romantic feeling warm

A romantic like pursuing
A romantic person's love or desire
A romantic is not enough
A romantic to light the fire

A romantic weaves the future
A romantic existence dreaming
A romantic longer separating
A romantic reality unfolding

A romantic for life
A romantic for death
A romantic on a projected stage
A romantic until the curtains close

16

Cosmic love, the orbs that define home or some other
conception of positionality and scale for the human element,
extending beyond does it transcend, if not limited to words,
energy transfer, moving in astral fluid, the universe is its
playground

17

A sucker for love not for how love is defined / maybe
'romance' would not be so far fetched / maybe too I have
internalized this view and we are mutually in the magnetic

pull / difficult to stop force in the absence of simultaneous
commitment / to tear down the walls and embrace like
'intelligent' animals

18

Keep-you-warm love, inexplicable longing
Sweet lying, some awkward redemption
Twisted dreams, veils eyes
Lips curled, silence and body rise
To li/ove is to lo/ive
Not to think about li/oving

19

Lost touch of the scope of love, the way that it keeps me
fighting to win an internal war that was waged long before
I was born, the way that love tells the artist to keep creating,
it tells me to keep living, to keep fighting

20

Sometimes it feels like I have been left for dead
Mechanically traversing loveless environments

But even where the human has privileged themselves the
   most
Always grows a li/ove inescapable

21

~~The lapping of shallow waves~~
~~Erodes my legs in familiar waters~~
~~The sand retains its shape~~
~~Brings me to my knees~~
~~Grinds my everyday to dust~~

Silhouette falling from the sky
My mind could be a beautiful space
Filled with what makes me lovely
Ending the romantic chase
Of some so-called wonderland

22

i i i i i i i i i i i i i i l o l o l o l o l o o o o o o o o v v v v v v v v v
ev e e e e e e e e e e e e ee e eeee e ee t t t t t h hh h h e e e e w
w a a a y y y y i i i i c a n n i ' m s o r r r y y y y y y y y y y y i f
s o o o m e t i m e s i t d o o e s s n t f e e e e l l l l ik e e e e n o
u g g g g h h h h

23

I grow more tired each day of scrolling through the details
of things, getting lost in the horrific specifics, the repetitive
fragments that separate and divide. I wonder if I love myself
enough to stop.

24

Dear words written on the page
I wish i could say goodbye
I do not love you
And you know why

25

The storms clearing, love
Washing you ashore on the other side
Of everything you have ever known

26

To love without judgment
Excites me in a way
I have never felt before

27

I'm tired of feeling less
When our love is more
But now that I am budding fruit
I'll let it rot
With the dead leaves
I leave behind

28

hungry   they tried to swallow me
      eat the peace that makes me whole   digested
'down to earth' they say   but where else
     should we be   my love

29

Sometimes I wonder what it would be like
To live in the absence I was led to believe
Was somehow in me

30

[some form of comfortable depth]

'Yeah i'm also aromantic'

'Oh.'

[regurgitated fallout]

31

I make love to you under the covers
Stitched to your mouth, it hurts to pull
Them out, untangle the mess
They made of you and I
But we are strong
And I love you enough to tell you
That you can

32

The repressed self
Is what we might call *feral*
I wonder what a love is
That is as well

33

Downstrung to the sea
The moon sings me songs as i walk
We are together

It all rests, existential threats
Subsists in huge push and pull
To feel my cyborg eyes crylove

34

I'm happy to not let romance go. Romance gave me nothing
and I have lost nothing without it, because it was never a
part of me.

35

in the vacuum of elevated surface structures
we might forget what it feels like to be loved by mud
i think many have forgotten

36

I love you enough
To tell you
That you misread my love
For romance, and it occurred to me then
The extent of the problem
Loveful expressions
Assumed to be indications of my affection
That looking through romantic eyes
So much is missed

37

I love the way you disfigure the grip of lovelessness
Your touch knows love's soft power to destroy

38

L_ve
foels
so lmpty
now
toat
wo're
Together

39
'What was love to them?'
'I couldn't tell'

'What was love to you?'
'Something that would make me cry

Pull tears from my skull
Fill up the insides

The trees, the ocean, the sky
That was love'

'How did they treat your love?'
'Like it was nothing'

40
My love will you . . . love me
As the atmosphere breaks
And the Earth makes aromantic love
with itself
And all things remake?

6

Notes from the Agender Refuge

noun: refuge

- *a condition of being safe or sheltered from pursuit, danger, or trouble*
- *something providing shelter*[1]

Note 1

There is a sense of calm that washes over you in a refuge, where you can embrace the silence. It might be lonely, and you will hear the reverberations of familiar calls to return back to the place from whence you came, but it is a shelter to pause and reflect.

In my own reflections, I learned that there was no longer a gender that I should try to define myself by. How could trying to embody such a word bring me any of the internal peace I required to move forward in the battle of life?

Rather, it was peace itself I needed – where I could *be* without the cisheteropatriarchal expectations and the violence they brought upon my body, my community, and the world. Knowing this goal to be unreachable in my lifetime and knowing words will always fall short, I still found a sort of refuge in *agender*. This was not because I was trying to be it, but because it was something I was not trying to be.

Gender is the eggshell
And I am breaking out

Note 2

I was assigned male at birth. I was socialized as 'male' and, therefore, I was conditioned to conform to standards of Western masculinity from a very young age. Almost everybody assigned male at birth underwent a similar socialization experience and process, which essentially involved the internalization of cisheteropatriarchal masculinity, policing everyone to meet its toxic and fragile expectations while being policed by others to remain within them.

This was the journey I was on as a presumed-to-be-heterosexual boy. When I expressed my love in ways marked as 'feminine' in my childhood, my love was suppressed and corrected back to what was deemed 'normal' for boys. This began as relatively subtle conditioning, yet became more pronounced throughout my adolescence, the period in which gender policing often accelerates tremendously among peers.

When I was young, gender transgressions could be excused as expressions of 'childhood innocence.' However, an adolescent or adult doing the same is apt to produce a more extreme reaction, as with age comes the assumption that the person 'should know better' than to transgress cisheteropatriarchy. If gendered expectations are solidified in childhood, they can become as rigid as daggers by adolescence and adulthood.

This resulted in confrontations marked by physical, verbal,

and psychological violence that repeatedly forced me to question my worth as a human being. Fearing a continuation of these consequences for defying the gendered expectations of the category of 'man,' I self-policed and constricted my own gender expressions as much as possible, pursuing in my adolescence the total elimination of what could be read as transgressions to the gender binary.

Under cisheteropatriarchy, I learned that almost nobody wants to be associated with a person perceived as a boy or man who does not conform to gender expectations. This froze much of my willingness to engage with others in social settings. All of the exhausting dimensions of gender made me feel very apathetic toward it and those who upheld its sanctity. Not really feeling attached to boyhood or manhood, while at the same time feeling indifferent to being socially 'read' as a man, I sought some refuge.

Eventually my disassociation from Western notions of manhood, and the gender binary I knew, led me to agenderness. I wondered how much of a role cisheteropatriarchal gender standards had in shaping my journey. Would I still have found resonance with agenderness if gender wasn't defined by cisheteropatriarchal or otherwise such rigid standards – if our gender visions had not been so clouded? I am always reminded that other worlds are possible.

Note 3

Agender is a relatively new identity, with reports on its first use as a reference to *being without gender* dating to 2000,[2] along with related terms *genderless* and *genderfree*.[3] I found the word *agender* in my process of disidentifying from the gender that had been imposed upon me from birth; the gender that I was conditioned to believe should 'fit' me. In my process of escaping the formations and (il)logics of gender that I had drowned in since I was young, *agender* offered me a place to rest. It became my refuge from gender.

The gender binary was like an assault on my body
Borders were erected through my brain
Man or woman
Sometimes I forget
Too bad others remind me

The modern colonial world is rife with gendered bombardments – expectations that the body is one's destiny or that gender categorization is essential. I have encountered others who have spoken to how *agender* was a place of rest or shelter for them from the intrusions gender expectations caused in their lives. Resting from the pursuit of applying or forcing ourselves to meet gender expectations provides us with an opportunity to reflect on who we are and who we might be without them. It is here, even if at first alone, where we may begin to nurture ourselves from the assault.

Note 4

Agender may be understood as a disidentification from gender; as a rejection or departure from gender. People may gravitate toward identifying as agender as a *response to* or *refusal of* the restrictive way gender has been dominantly imagined.

Agender people may discover that they could always see through gender in a way that others could not. Gender performativity may have consistently appeared obvious to them, even if they did not have the language to convey this at the time. Where cisheteropatriarchy has not influenced attitudes and behaviors – as limited as those places may be because of colonialism and the pursuit to replicate Western formations – *agender* may not be seen as necessary, applicable, or desirable. The contemporary movement to deconstruct gender reflects the 'growing pains' of expanding a system that has disastrously failed to adequately grasp human experiences, too limited to be sustainable or livable.[4]

So if I say I am *agender*, I say it as a statement against a particular structuring of gender that was imposed upon myself and the world as a 'colonized' person; to, in other words, reject this imposition on my body, on my mind, and on my spirit. It is to place myself in this placeholder.

Note 5

Agenderness gives us space to understand how we exist in the world without confining ourselves to the gender binary and its expectations. However, even when we find refuge in *agender*, we remain subjected to the binary based on how our bodies are interpreted. Heidi Samuelson addressed this in a piece for *AZE*: 'It doesn't matter what I say or do or insist on, people are going to gender me as a woman anyway because of how I look, because of how they were socialized.'[5] For myself, if I am viewed as desirable or undesirable, it is largely because of how I am interpreted in relation to what is deemed (un)desirable for a man within the confines of Western masculinity.

Even within queer spaces, desirability can still function through certain gendered expectations. In an article entitled 'Thoughts on Being a Fem Agender: And Never Feeling Queer Enough' for *AZE*, Shei identified how gender neutrality is coded through a standardized appearance, even within queer spaces: "It took me a long time to realize that androgyny did not mean being white, thin, heavily-tattooed/pierced, and only wearing 'masculine' clothes." Working to avoid the practice of immediately gendering how we look can deconstruct the gender stereotypes we attach to our appearances.[6] This requires a conscious effort by society to unlearn gender assumptions that are deeply embedded within us as a result of media narratives, familial pressures, and general social conditioning. Knowing the immensity of this task, we should not put the pressure on ourselves of striving for perfection or being consumed by the emotional labor of it all, but do what we can to move forward and remember to rest in the refuges we may come across along the way.

Note 6

The space for a gender
That is not yet created
That was subsumed underneath
The cisheteropatriarchal tide
The rage at such a system
And its discontents
Reverberates everywhere
But from my shelter
I still hear the roots
Growing, breaking down
All the shit
Keeps me alive

Note 7

In the latter half of the twentieth century, there were emerging critiques over the idea that "man's anatomy is his destiny," as published in a briefing for a US Supreme Court case in 1970.[7] At the same time, protectors of cisheteropatriarchy and the static nature of the Western gender binary, such as Gerard J. M. van den Aardweg, professed that "rather than encourage gender nonconformity" or a "different gender identity" than that assigned at birth, families and institutions should continue "to treat a boy as a boy and a girl as a girl" through advising "healthy parental attitudes and child-rearing practices with respect to the child's gender role."[8]

The lingering power of sexology discourses pathologizing disconformity from Western cisheteropatriarchy was rearing its head, as it does today. The architects of sexology in the nineteenth century proudly referred to gender binary distinctions as proof of white supremacy and "civilization."[9] Richard von Krafft-Ebing, author of *Psychopathia Sexualis*, asserted that "the higher the anthropological development of the race, the stronger the contrasts between man and woman, and vice versa."[10] In 1898, Annie L. Mearkle identified that this distinction was predicated on European men's belief that women were naturally inferior and similar to the 'savage' or the child: "Men say we are so because we are women, not because we are young." Mearkle herself believed in the sexological narrative that the distinction between man and woman was an indicator of white supremacy: "differentiation means superiority and it is itself an effect of development." Thus, she cautioned others over women who "wish to be wiser" yet fail to "see that the chief duty of woman is to be interesting to man."[11]

In his book *The Philosophy of Civilization* (1923), Rutherford Hamilton Towner wrote that "the adult savage is still called a child of the forest" – an infantilizing characterization that implies that living in a closely bound interrelationship with nature is developmentally inferior to being, or rather believing, that one is in control of nature. Comparatively, Towner argued that differences of both physical and psychical nature "exist in equal or increased degree in civilized mankind," believing a woman to be civilized when her "physical adaptability to motherhood is animated by humility, duty, obedience, religion, necessity, or abnegation." These differences were said to be calculable with "mathematical accuracy," again reflecting how the language of 'scientific' discourse was used to assert the alleged superiority of white supremacy and colonial cisheteropatriarchy.[12]

Since the gender binary was deemed to be a product and representation of human 'evolution,' upholding its status was and remains entwined with notions of protecting and advancing 'civilization.' This meant enforcing women's submission and men's domination through Chrisitan institutions, a dynamic that itself was rooted in the European practice of accusing and violently targeting women to be 'witches' for hundreds of years, often for their knowledge of medicinal plants and interrelationship with nature, that predated the colonialism of Turtle Island and Abya Yala. This 'witch-hunt' in Europe was subsequently enforced in the colonies via such apparatuses as the Inquisition, severely altering gender dynamics and humanity's ways of perceiving and being with nature throughout the world. This also meant eliminating people who Western researchers have more recently referred to as 'third gender' via gendercide. People who did not conform to the gender binary have long been targeted by people claiming to be more civilized than others, such as Christian missionaries and colonizers who traveled to Turtle Island and beyond. In one early encounter between a missionary and a Indigenous person who did not conform to European gender constructs (now conceptualized as two-spirit), the missionary reported:

> We place our trust in God and expect that these accursed people will disappear with the growth of the missions. The abominable vice will be eliminated to the extent that the Catholic faith

and all the other virtues are firmly implanted there, for the glory of God and the benefit of those poor ignorants.[13]

Unfortunately this was not an isolated case, but stands as evidence of a larger 'holy crusade' to commit gendercide through the violence of missionization and colonial governance. Scott Lauria Morgensen wrote that the targeting of Indigenous gender and sexual variance was done to "teach both colonial and Indigenous subjects the relational terms of colonial heteropatriarchy." Violence was used to force colonized populations, increasingly under the surveillance of colonizers, to conform to Western gender expectations. Indigenous men were enlisted by colonial cisheteropatriarchy to "defend colonial sexual morality" in their own communities.[14] This meant that people who were once accepted as integral members with well-defined roles were now rejected, ostracized, and, sometimes, concealed by their communities.

What has come to be defined as *queerness* was thus separated from the whole of humanity through colonization. Yvette Abrahams reflected on the role European colonialism and Christianization played in not only imposing cisheteropatriarchal structures onto Indigenous peoples, but attempting to alter core aspects of their worldviews:

So we didn't actually when colonialism first came have an idea of sin or evil. We now 500 years later have had aptly demonstrated to us that yes sin exists and evil is real. We still struggle with the notion that it could be inborn. So what colonial religions asked of us in relation to LGBTIQ, you know firstly the notion that you could be born sinful that you could be born in some way wrong made absolutely no sense because now what this religion was asking of us was to reject

our own children, who were made in the image of God [. . .]
Our very pre-colonial culture was so diverse and so accepting
that the notion of queerness in fact didn't exist. We didn't
think of gender as a binary because we were people very
closely related to nature and located in nature [. . .][15]

The framing that queerness is 'against nature' then is actually
unnatural. It is just the pursuit of cisheteropatriarchy, often
fortified by some notion of religious purity or sanctity, that
obscures this truth. This is one of the central arguments against
queerness; that nature only intended for what is termed 'heterosexuality' between a cisgender 'masculine' man and a
cisgender 'feminine' woman. If this were true, why would
queer people continue to be born, generation after generation?
Religious groups often explain this by referring to queer
people as *inherently* sinful or being born into a life where they
must unrelentingly fight against their queerness, which Abrahams recognizes as a *division* that has been imposed on humanity
through colonial violence.

Rooted in this history, threats against cisheteropatriarchy
are still essentially framed as assaults on 'civilization' and
'order,' although not always using such obvious language as
was regularly employed in the nineteenth or early twentieth
centuries. Appeals to 'science' to uphold cisheteropatriarchy
remain present. For the colonial mind, an agender world,
where gender 'does not matter,' thus appears to be a dangerous 'unscientific' regression. It is a surrender to the 'wild' or
chaos of the unknown – *His* lack of control – that is the colonizer's greatest fear.

the gender breakdown
is incomplete

for 'queers' like me
who were set to be eradicated
as the 'abominations'
we were
in the eyes of missionaries
who came to this land
and defiled the bodies
of women, men,
and children
to make
a 'better' gender
out of them
did their stomachs ever churn
like mine does now?
did their minds attack their bodies
or tell them to disappear?
from the mess they made
i wonder
if they wondered
at all

Note 8

To decolonize gender is to deconstruct the dominant terms gender is framed in and (re)focus on the acceptance of individuals who have been ostracized by its institutionalization. Through this work, the potential of interconnectedness to bring about communal strength is effectively unlimited. It is only our limited visions that keep us from unlocking it. This was spoken about in a 2018 talk by Wade Blevins:

> Our beliefs are centered around a fire. We believe that fire was given to us by God in the beginning of things and we were

told that as long as we kept that fire going we would continue
to exist as Cherokee people. One time he [Benny Smith] told
me, "Everybody has a place at this fire," and he said [. . .]
"Until our transgender people once again are able to stand at
that fire and take those places, our fire has become diminished
and weak because not everyone is there, and until we create
that space again, our fire is not as strong as it could be."[16]

Adopting an *agender lens* allows us to imagine futures where
gender does not have to divide us. As it stands now, there are
whole populations of people who are prevented or dissuaded
from standing at a family's or community's hearth because of
the continued reign of colonial cisheteropatriarchy. I take
refuge sometimes from the enormous pressure of thinking
about all that is lost from this disunity, but know that we
must remember to move forward.

Note 9
All things coming together
Going through it
Entering into the expanse
Never to be the same
Drowned in possibility
Erase the lines
Release the imagination

Note 10
So much about how gender is defined, understood, and
approached fixates on our physical bodies. As Chrystos stated,
"the mind has no gender."[17] The belief that the origins of
gender are found in the physical body dictates that it resides
solely in the material realm rather than as an expression of

spirit. The spirit, as "the common life force within and between all beings," is generally rejected in the dominant Western worldview as "superstition, folk belief, or New Age delusion."[18] The spirit cannot be 'rationally' or empirically measured by separable ways of thinking.

In the modern colonial world, gender is determined for a person without any knowledge of who they are internally. Our bodies become our destiny as we are set on a path of becoming either 'men' or 'women.' Alternatively, our gender could be determined through careful observation and communal input. Gender could be a guided process that aligns with our interiority rather than an imposed designation. This would free gender from the carceral (il)logics that dominate Western life, making it no longer a prison that we are born into, but a force that can empower our interconnectedness and, thus, our communities.

For the time being, agender can be a refuge for us.

Note 11

Xicanx is not a refusal of gender, but abandons the mindset of conceiving one's gender, sexuality, ancestry, and worldview as static and separable. This is reflected in the redundancy of calling myself both *agender* and *Xicanx*, the latter of which already symbolically orients the self external to the Western gender binary with its inclusion of -x (as well as with a decolonial orientation that is symbolically reflected in the first X-).

To use the term *Xicanx* in lieu of a gender identification then loosens the modern colonial worldview's hold, not only over gender identity, but how identity overall is *expected* to function as a list of separable yet potentially overlapping social categories or terms that reflect or represent the internal capacities of the individuals who use them.

What is being Xicanx to me
But being in-between, some place
Where the past is the present and the present is x
The clown, strangeness, a 'mess'
But I have learned, i guess
That the X that marks the spot
Where I am and i am not

Note 12
In my refuge i remake a gender
Mold it from the clay, i awake
then crumble to dust, back to earth

In my refuge is a looking glass
To see a world ungendered
Waiting to spill open, break

Genders fall to pieces
As real as they are fake
In this endless space

Conclusion

Ending the pursuit has been a conceptual reference point in my life over the years. It became a tool for me to reflect on the myriad of ways colonial (il)logics have trained us to engage in pursuits that, at their core, are detrimental to our wellbeing. As I identified the multilayered and multidimensional nature of these pursuits, I recognized that, despite their overbearing presence in our lives, without the proper tools or inspiration, they could remain unexposed or unopposed.

One of my purposes for writing this book was to make the work of *ending* feel urgent on an individual, communal, and species-level scale. To demonstrate that the urgency to divest from separable thinking could not be more apparent and needed in our times, as Theresa Yugar, Juan Tavárez, and Alan Barrera remind us:

> The statistical reality is that the rational, logical, capitalist, consumerist, industrial, and 'enlightened' West is the main cause of climate change [. . .] This growth economy, powered by capitalist multinational corporations and consumerist lifestyles, is simply not sustainable. If we are to successfully address climate change, we must be transparent about its sources.[1]

Since our ideas of what is 'rational,' 'logical,' and 'enlight-ened' have also been misconstrued, to start the arduous process of deconstructing our (mis)education requires a recognition of not only the genocide of Indigenous peoples throughout the world, but the epistemicide of Indigenous *ways of knowing*. Elewani Ramugondo spoke of the importance of recognizing this simultaneous genocide and epistemicide: "So you don't put a veneer over an ugly history and present the current as if it happened by itself." [2]

Ending the pursuit can guide us to collectively celebrate our interconnectedness, but to do so requires the fortitude to exist in an unsettled state of being. It requires stretching and growing, challenging our perspectives, and facing difficult truths. It was the aspiration to speak to interconnectedness that guided me through the process of writing this book; to stay true to my 'queer' decolonial worldview that aligned with my dreams for a better world. There were many ups and downs amidst it all. Yet, being in this flux state allows for the greater ability to sustain ourselves in the modern colonial world, and also to experience the joys of life that grow through the cracks in the colonial concrete. Looking inward is essential to forming and actualizing our own sense of iden-tity, disentangled from colonial pursuits, especially for the 'colonized': "To acquire freedom in the decolonized and delineated order, the colonized must break their silence and struggle to retake possession of their humanity and identity," noted James (Sákéj) Youngblood Henderson. [3]

Ending the pursuit of Western expectations of 'sexuality,' 'romance,' 'attraction,' and 'gender' is what this book calls for us to recognize so that we may end our investment in confin-ing ourselves within the limits of cisheteropatriarchal (il)logics (and thus place ourselves in alignment with the ever-changing universe). It is to end the pursuit of ordering the world by cisheteropatriarchal standards; the pursuit of finding conditions to explain 'impossible' challenges to our worldview; the pursuit of defining an identity by strict terms and policing ourselves with such definitions; the pursuit of labeling and attempting to legitimate what is 'natural' and 'unnatural' via 'scientific' discourses; the pursuit of upholding romantic love at the top of a hierarchy above other forms of relationality; the pursuit of finding sexual meanings in all forms and expressions of attraction; the pursuit of maintaining the colonial gender binary.

A life journey does not simply end with *ending* these pursuits. Rather, it continues in the stream of life when one feels what it means to be 'untethered.' It begins from the understanding that, as written by Lisa Grayshield, Marilyn Begay, and Laura L. Luna, "life is a journey of cleansing and transformation, from the most basic of human needs for clean water, air, nourishment and warmth; to the fundamental knowing of one's most inner truth as an individual expression of a whole."[4]

Holistically speaking, ending the pursuit requires a transformation of 'life as we know it' under modern coloniality – a transition from the domination of separable ways of knowing and being to interconnected ways of knowing and being. However, since our life trajectories are deeply entangled in larger structures and systems that depend on the pursuit to maintain 'life as we know it' – ultimately for greed, not for our collective wellbeing – we are tasked with moving forward, knowing that we are being misled, which may initially generate uncertainty and instability. Yet disidentifying from the pursuit makes rooting ourselves in interconnectedness possible.

Community support can help nurture us in the disidentification process. Through this work we can envision other
worlds or '*otros mundos*' that exist "beyond the narrow confines of the nation";[5] to imagine and enact "other ways of
being in the world, and ultimately new worlds."[6] For many
years of my life, I have pursued 'fitting in' for the purpose of
achieving what I thought would be happiness; an existence
where I could be well liked and 'safe' from ostracization.
This meant that I expended time and energy in pursuing
ideals with which I did not align. I was trying to erase myself
in the pursuit of conformity. This involved: being trained
in the church to use Christianity as a shield to conceal my
'queerness;' trained to believe a 'fantasy heritage' of the
place I called 'home;' and trained to aspire to standards of
'success' and 'comfort' in colonial capitalist society. This is
what was defined as the 'pursuit of happiness' – so long as
how we define 'happiness' did not challenge the established
(dis)order.

Rather than as a pursuit of something – a process through
which we drain our time and energy through chasing – what
if we thought of a life force that we can feed to nurture us
through the journey of life, much like we must feed the soil
in order to feed the plant? That which keeps me living, not
existing, in modern coloniality I choose to define as *the quazar
inside*, to signal toward our inherent spiritual connection with
the cosmos as well as the fusion of queerness and azeness
(hence being spelled quazar) within us: how our insides
simultaneously reflect what is claimed to *not supposed to be there*
but is (queerness) and what is not there but is 'supposed' to be
(azeness). The quazar is the spiritual source that feeds us to
express, to create, to grow, to love, to interconnect, to try, to
feel. The ways in which we become in tune with ourselves,

the ways in which we learn to feed the quazar, are what nurture us to encounter, to face, reality.

Rather than an identity, the quazar is the place where I simultaneously come from, am present, and am going – like the soil of the Earth we come from, are made of, and return to. In *Beyond Settler Time: Temporal Sovereignty and Indigenous Self-Determination* (2017), Mark Rifkin identifies that there are "varied temporal formations that have their own rhythms" that are engaged in "potentially divergent processes of becoming." He poses the question: "What does it mean to consider Native temporalities as having their own flow – as coherent yet changing, affected by other flows but not the same as them?"[7] The modern colonial world is obsessed with absorption, with believing itself as having the 'civilized' right to consume and order everything into one way of perceiving, thinking, acting, and being in the world. The idea of the 'melting pot' or gentrification, of transforming diversity into a bland mush of sameness, reflects this pursuit of absorption. This perception also emerges in the belief that Western identity labels, terms, and classification systems can and should be universally applied.

The labels *asexual, aromantic, agender*, and many others that we may use to label our 'sexuality,' 'romance,' 'attraction,' and 'gender,' have been formed through this matrix. They exist in relation to a host of other identity labels and general beliefs about sex, romance, attraction, and gender that are deeply naturalized in Western culture, having become the building blocks many of us depend on to label ourselves and others. As Kenny Ramos identifies, "oftentimes in the LGBTQ+ community, there is a focus on these labels that are all still colonial labels, and they're all rooted in a Western colonial idea of gender and sexuality."[8] Even as the norms and expectations are increasingly being challenged and breaking open, the legacies of the colonial root remain present, yet often go unrecognized. This is not to say that asexual, aromantic, and agender identity are any less 'valid' than any other labels – a major contribution of this book was to demonstrate how Western expectations of sexuality, romance, attraction, and gender are both limited and limiting, based in hierarchy and reinforcing colonialism. Rather, it means developing a critical consciousness of what trajectory these labels have emerged within and asking the questions: Where is this trajectory headed? What is it pursuing?

To navigate such a task requires an awareness of how we have been conditioned to adopt a separable worldview, so that we can form an interconnected worldview that avoids the pitfalls of separable thinking. This includes the pursuit to strictly compartmentalize identity. As such, if someone were to ask me if I identify as asexual, aromantic, or agender, I could answer, 'Yes . . . within the Western worldview.' To engage in this wordplay may seem unnecessary. However, it challenges the assumed universality of the Western worldview and forefronts how multiple worldviews can exist simultaneously. It does not delegitimize asexual, aromantic, and agender identity, but rather makes known what paradigm they exist or are rooted within. It symbolically invites the end of the pursuit to attempt to crunch and separate all of our existences into a universal model, embracing a pluriversal approach to our existence in which we can begin to "think beyond the idea of a single world, a single reality, a single form of the possible." [9]

Feeding the quazar helps me to be present amidst the chaos of the pursuit of uniformity and conformity; to be embraced by the earth that we grow from, fed by everything around us that is an embodiment of spiritual energy; to surrender the obsession with separable thinking, because it only leads to misery and chaos – like a plant that hypothetically attempts to separate itself from the soil. Ending the pursuit is thus an acceptance that we exist as all life does, as children of the universe – to express ourselves through occasional blooms, produce fruit, drop leaves, feed everything through our decomposition and nourishing of the soil; to nourish life in our own life, relationality, and death. This does not mean ignoring life in a delusion or to attempt to isolate or define ourselves as 'superior,' but to accept this relationality, embrace root growth and interconnectivity with all that's around us. If our lives can illuminate the world, send vibrations outward that are beneficial to thriving life, to all our relations, then that is *ending the pursuit*.

Characteristic of all of the human-subject's attempts to control reality through violence, there is a fundamental dis-respect and disregard for the Earth by assuming an authority to speak for everything and dictate life through one's own assumptions of what is 'unnatural' and 'natural.' In 2018, a short street interview in China (translated into English) went as follows:

> *Interviewer:* If your child came out of the closet, how
> would you feel about that?
> *Interviewee:* I'd say let nature take its course.
> *Interviewer:* So you wouldn't interfere.
> *Interviewee:* No, I wouldn't.[10]

The interviewee's response illustrated a worldview in which the individual does not prioritize their judgment or make assumptions based on the belief that they have the authority to speak or act for nature. While the phrase 'let nature take its course' was used in reference to gayness, in applying this mindset to asexuality, aromanticism, and agenderness, we can see how the acknowledgement of the power of nature can decenter our own judgment; our own attempts to compartmentalize or 'rationalize,' even if the reasons cannot always be understood by our smallness in comparison to the immensity of nature's power.

Such a perspective reminds us that the boundaries we have established for ourselves are less 'natural' than we may have been conditioned to believe; it returns our focus back to our interconnectedness. On the journey to reclaiming ourselves from the pursuit, the universe reminds us that we do not have to pursue, but *let go.*

Cisheteropatriarchy is a curse
Pressures us to feel weak
Tells us not to speak
So we must scream

Notes

Introduction

1 *Xicanx* is a term I use to describe myself for several reasons simultaneously: as a person whose ancestry is both 'Native American' (indigenous to Turtle Island) and 'European' (indigenous to 'Europe'), as a person who does not feel comfortable forcing themselves to conform to the gender expectations of the settler colonial binary, and as a person who feels a commitment to social justice.

2 Putting queerness in quotes is done to symbolically remind us that the notion only exists because of the problematization of people who do not conform to the expectations of colonial cisheteropatriarchy. Putting queer in quotes also signals toward a future where the term is no longer needed – the same of which can be said of other categorical terms.

3 Lee Maracle, 'Connection between Violence against the Earth and Violence against Women,' Indigenous Peoples' Solidarity Movement Ottawa, YouTube, August 28, 2012, https://www.youtube.com/watch?v=VdxJYhbTvYw&ab_channel=IPSMO.

4 This included many writers and artists, such as Paula Gunn Allen, Chrystos, and Lisa Grayshield.

5 Throughout this book, these identities are listed in this way to reflect how I encountered them. It is not to hierarchize them or make one out to be a symptom of another.

6 Sonal Kulkarni-Joshi and S. Imtiaz Hasnain, 'Northern perspectives on language and society in India,' in *Colonial and Decolonial Linguistics:*

Knowledges and Epistemes, ed. Ana Deumert, Anne Storch, and Nick Shepherd (New York: Oxford University Press, USA, 2021), 25; 'Since the 1500s we have increasingly been living in a *modern colonial world*. From the Renaissance on there was a development of a narrative of progress, development, organization, and doing good for the world. The colonial narrative vis-à-vis language, which was constructed mainly by the Europeans, finds expression in the myth of the Tower of Babel, which marks the beginning of modernity's glorification of homogeneity and uniformity' (emphasis added).

7 Pam Maraldo and Mary Samost, 'Gender and Leadership,' in *Nursing Leadership: A Concise Encyclopedia*, ed. Harriet R. Feldman (New York: Springer Publishing Company, 2011), 170–172.

8 Other is in reference to the philosophical concept of Othering, or the act of relegating certain people to be innately different from ourselves.

9 David Bohm, *Wholeness and the Implicate Order* (London: Psychology Press, 2002 [1980]), 158.

10 Campaigns to 'Kill the Indian, Save the Man,' for instance, illustrate how European colonizers were keenly aware of the differences between Western and Indigenous worldviews, especially concerning what constituted 'Man' vs. 'Indian.'

11 Armida de la Garza, 'Aboriginal Digitalities: Indigenous Peoples and New Media,' in *The Digital Arts and Humanities: Neogeography, Social Media and Big Data Integrations and Applications*, ed. Charles Travis and Alexander V. Lünen (Basingstoke: Springer, 2018), 56.

12 Rodolfo F. Acuña, *Assault on Mexican American Collective Memory, 2010–2015: Swimming with Sharks* (Lanham: Rowman & Littlefield, 2017), 10.

13 *Turtle Island* and *Abya Yala* are more Indigenous-centered terms that are used here in place of the terms *North America* and *South America*.

14 Qwo-Li Driskill, *Asegi Stories: Cherokee Queer and Two-Spirit Memory* (Tucson: University of Arizona Press, 2016), 23.

15 Silvia R. Cusicanqui, *Ch'ixinakax utxiwa: una reflexión sobre prácticas y discursos descolonizadores* (Tinta Limón, 2010), 19.

16 Rodolfo F. Acuña, *Assault on Mexican American Collective Memory* (Lanham: Rowman & Littlefield, 2017), vii.

17 Eve Tuck and K. Wayne Yang, 'Decolonization is not a metaphor,' *Decolonization: Indigeneity, Education & Society* 1, no. 1 (2012).

18 Greg Sarris, *Mabel McKay: Weaving the Dream* (Oakland: University of California Press, 2013 [1994]), 2. Mabel McKay stated in a 1994 lecture on her basket weaving: 'It's no such thing as art. It's spirit. My grandma never taught me nothing about the baskets. Only the spirit trained me. [. . .] I only follow the dream. That's how I learn.'

1 Coming Out of the Impossible

1 Rahul Rao, *Out of Time: The Queer Politics of Postcoloniality* (New York: Oxford University Press, 2020), xix.

2 While asexuality has become defined as *the lack of sexual attraction*, within the social imagination, when the term *asexual* is initially confronted, it is often interpreted as *the lack of sexual desire or sexual drive*.

3 Shannon Deery, 'No love for aromantic flag flying,' *Herald Sun* – via Pressreader.com, last modified February 26, 2021, https://www.press reader.com/australia/herald-sun/20210226/281595243255300

4 Vera Papisova, 'What It Means to Identify As Agender,' *Teen Vogue*, last modified January 20, 2016, https://www.teenvogue.com/story/ what-is-agender

5 Jie Yang, '"We Are Not Broken": The Struggles of Being an Aromantic Allosexual,' Heroica, last modified May 28, 2022, https:// www.heroica.co/identity/we-are-not-broken-the-struggles-of-being-an-aromantic-allosexual

6 'Social Anxiety and Asexuality,' Asexuality Archive, last modified September 6, 2015, https://www.asexualityarchive.com/social-anxiety-and-asexuality/

7 Jessica Vazquez, 'Coming Out Twice: On Being Gay and Asexual in a World Without Representation,' Autostraddle, last modified April 17, 2021, https://www.autostraddle.com/coming-out-twice-on-being-gay-and-asexual-in-a-world-without-representation/

8 Justin J. Lehmiller, *The Psychology of Human Sexuality* (Hoboken: John Wiley & Sons, 2017), 250.

9 Meghna Mehra, '10 Things Asexual People Are Tired Of Hearing,' Feminism in India, last modified October 22, 2019, https://feminis-minindia.com/2019/10/23/10-things-asexual-people-tired-hearing/

10 Lucy Wallis, 'What is It Like to Be Asexual?,' BBC News, last modified January 17, 2012, https://www.bbc.com/news/magazine-16552173

11 Jade Nicole, 'Find the Right Person,' AZE, last modified August 20, 2018, https://azejournal.com/article/2018/8/13/find-the-right-person

12 Myra T. Johnson, 'Asexual and Autoerotic Women: Two Oppressed Groups,' in *The Sexually Oppressed*, ed. Harvey L. Gochros and Jean S. Gochros (New York City: Association Press, 1977), 96–109.

13 Luke Brunning and Natasha McKeever, 'Asexuality,' *Journal of Applied Philosophy* 38, no. 3 (October 2020), https://onlinelibrary.wiley.com/doi/full/10.1111/japp.12472

14 Mark Carrigan, 'There's more to life than sex? Difference and commonality within the asexual community,' *Sexualities* 14, no. 4 (2011): 473, doi:10.1177/1363460711406462

15 Yasmin Benoit, '"I'll Never Fall in Love and That's OK": What It Means to Be Aromantic,' Stylist, last modified February 21, 2022, https://www.stylist.co.uk/relationships/aromantic-love/624674

16 Namrata K, 'Experiencing Love As An Aromantic Asexual (Aroace) Person,' Feminism in India, last modified December 27, 2020, https://feminisminindia.com/2020/12/28/experiencing-love-aromantic-asexual-aroace-person/

17 Rosie Swash, 'Among the asexuals,' *The Guardian*, last modified February 25, 2012, https://www.theguardian.com/lifeandstyle/2012/feb/26/among-the-asexuals

18 Nikki Hayfield, *Bisexual and Pansexual Identities: Exploring and Challenging Invisibility and Invalidation* (London: Routledge, 2020), 2–3.

19 C. J. Bishop, 'A mystery wrapped in an enigma – asexuality: a virtual discussion,' *Psychology and Sexuality* 4, no. 2 (May 2013): 195–206, doi: 10.1080/19419899.2013.774168

20 Ibid.

21 'Ace Week 2021 – Older Aces,' The Ace and Aro Advocacy Project, last modified October 26, 2021, https://taaap.org/2021/10/26/ace-week-21-older-aces/

22 Allo is short for *allosexual*, which is a term used to refer to a person who experiences sexual attraction in an assumed-to-be normal way.

23 Cody, 'Ace Week 2021 – Older Aces,' The Ace and Aro Advocacy Project, last modified October 26, 2021, https://taaap.org/2021/10/26/ace-week-21-older-aces/

24 Bianca Fileborn, 'Sexual Assault and Justice for Older Women: A Critical Review of the Literature,' *Trauma, Violence, & Abuse* 18, no. 5 (2016): 502, doi:10.1177/1524838016641666

25 The challenge here then is one of worldview, to embrace transformation and end the pursuit of binary thinking and the (il)logics of separability.

26 Eunjung Kim, 'Asexuality in disability narratives,' *Sexualities* 14, no. 4 (2011): 488, doi:10.1177/1363460711406463

27 Alyssa N. Clark and Corinne Zimmerman, 'Concordance Between Romantic Orientations and Sexual Attitudes: Comparing Allosexual and Asexual Adults,' *Archives of Sexual Behavior* 51, no. 4 (2022): doi:10.1007/s10508-021-02194-3

28 Hannah Moulton, 'Somewhere on the A-Spectrum: Agender, aromantic and asexual people face misconceptions, aggression,' *Daily Beacon*, last modified October 8, 2015, https://www.utdailybeacon. com/news/somewhere-on-the-a-spectrum-agender-aromantic-and-asexual-people-face-misconceptions-aggression/article_c3ada048-6d60-11e5-821c-db75108bfbc3.html

29 Ibid.

30 Paisley Gilmour, '3 People on What Aromantic Means to Them,' *Cosmopolitan*, last modified February 24, 2021, https://www.cosmo-politan.com/uk/love-sex/relationships/a23304501/aromantic/

31 Eunjung Kim, 'Asexuality in disability narratives,' *Sexualities* 14, no. 4 (2011): 483, doi:10.1177/1363460711406463

32 Paul Chappell, 'Troubling the socialisation of the sexual identities of youth with disabilities: Lessons for sexuality and HIV pedagogy,' in Francis D. A. (Ed.), *Sexuality, Society & Pedagogy*, (2014): 111–112. African Sun Media.

33 Lindokuhle Ubisi, 'De/coloniality, disabled sexualities, and anti-oppressive education: a review of Southern African literature,' *South African Journal of Psychology* 51, no. 1 (2020): doi:10.1177/0081246320956419

34 Anonymous, 'Not a Dirty Word – Being Disabled and Asexual,' SBS, last modified July 26, 2016, https://www.sbs.com.au/topics/ pride/agenda/article/2016/07/26/not-dirty-word-being-disabled-and-asexual

35 Courtney Lane, 'Why I'm Founding Disabled Ace Day,' Ace Week, last modified October 27, 2021, https://aceweek.org/stories/why-i-m-founding-disabled-ace-day

36 Charli Clement, 'I'm Not Responsible for the Misconception That All Disabled People Are Asexual,' The Unwritten, last modified April 6, 2021, https://www.theunwritten.co.uk/2021/04/06/im-not-responsible-for-the-misconception-that-all-disabled-people-are-asexual/

37 Courtney Lane, 'Why I'm Founding Disabled Ace Day,' Ace Week, last modified October 27, 2021, https://aceweek.org/stories/why-i-m-founding-disabled-ace-day

38 Aroace is a term to refer to a person who is both asexual and aromantic.

39 'ASAW 2022 – Disabled and Neurodivergent Aros,' The Ace and Aro Advocacy Project, last modified February 23, 2022, https://taaap.org/2022/02/23/asaw-22-disabled-neurodivergent-aros/

40 Ibid.

41 'Gender Identity: Is It a Mental Disorder?,' HCA Virginia, last modified October 10, 2019, https://hcavirginia.com/blog/entry/gender-identity-is-it-a-mental-disorder-

42 'Gender Dysphoria Diagnosis,' American Psychiatric Association, last modified November 2017, https://www.psychiatry.org/psychiatrists/diversity/education/transgender-and-gender-nonconforming-patients/gender-dysphoria-diagnosis

43 'Interactive Map: Gender-Diverse Cultures,' PBS Independent Lens, last modified April 21, 2022, https://www.pbs.org/independentlens/content/two-spirits_map-html/

44 Sean C. Murphy et al., 'The Role of Overconfidence in Romantic Desirability and Competition,' *Personality and Social Psychology Bulletin* 41, no. 8 (2015): 1036, doi:10.1177/0146167215588754

45 José E. Muñoz, *Cruising Utopia: The Then and There of Queer Futurity* (New York: NYU Press, 2009), 98.

46 Aasha B. Foster et al., 'Personal agency disavowed: Identity construction in asexual women of color,' *Psychology of Sexual Orientation and Gender Diversity* 6, no. 2 (2019): 128, doi:10.1037/sgd0000310.

47 Anais Rivero, 'Asexual People of Color On Their Experiences,' *Affinity Magazine*, last modified June 4, 2017, https://affinitymagazine.us/2017/06/04/asexual-people-of-color-on-their-experiences/

48 Ibid.

49 Foster et al., 'Personal agency disavowed: Identity construction in asexual women of color,' 133.

50 Danyi, '"You're Such a Waste": Too Attractive to Be Asexual,' *AZE*, last modified August 15, 2018, https://azejournal.com/article/2018/8/1/youre-such-a-waste-too-attractive-to-be-asexual

51 Sarah Doan-Minh, 'Corrective Rape: An Extreme Manifestation of Discrimination and the State's Complicity in Sexual Violence,' *Hastings Women's Law Journal* 30, no. 1 (Winter 2019): 174, https://repository.uchastings.edu/hwlj/vol30/iss1/8

52 Melissa, 'On Shedding Shame: Embracing My Asexuality,' *AZE*, last modified April 1, 2018, https://azejournal.com/article/2018/4/1/melissa-on-shedding-shame-embracing-my-asexuality

53 Sarah E. S. Sinwell, 'Aliens and Asexuality: Media Representation, Queerness, and Asexual Visibility,' in *Asexualities: Feminist and Queer Perspectives*, ed. K. J. Cerankowski and M. Milks (New York; Oxfordshire: Routledge, 2014), 166.

54 WebMD Editorial Contributors, 'What Does Aromantic Mean?,' WebMD, last modified November 24, 2020, https://www.webmd.com/sex/what-does-aromantic-mean

55 Josh Salisbury, 'Meet the Aromantics: "I'm Not Cold – I Just Don't Have Any Romantic Feelings,"' *Guardian*, last modified November 25, 2017, https://www.theguardian.com/lifeandstyle/2017/oct/11/meet-the-aromantics-not-cold-dont-have-romantic-feelings-sex

56 Logan Plonski, '7 Facts You Should Know About Aromantic People,' Them, last modified February 23, 2018, https://www.them.us/story/facts-you-should-know-about-aromantic-people

57 Jodi Tandet, '5 Quick Tips for Being Inclusive of Asexual Students on Campus—Plus 5 Myths You Need to Forget,' Modern Campus Presence, last modified June 11, 2019, https://www.presence.io/blog/5-quick-tips-for-being-inclusive-of-asexual-students-on-campus-plus-5-myths-you-need-to-forget/

58 Dawy Rkasnuam, 'Stop Assuming Everyone Wants a Partner: 5 Ways You're Erasing Asexual & Aromantic People and What to Do Instead,' The Body Is Not An Apology, last modified May 22, 2018, https://thebodyisnotanapology.com/magazine/5-ways-your-erasing-asexual-aromantic-people-and-what-to-say-instead/

59 AUREA Team, 'Advice on Coming Out As Aromantic,' AUREA, last modified January 17, 2020, https://www.aromanticism.org/en/news-feed/coming-out-advice

60 'Productivity' is commonly cited as a benefit of the cisheteropatriarchal formation, with the assumption being that human beings are best *reproduced* as monocultures – with uniformity, separation, and a hyperfocus on improving production despite harmful effects to the Earth and all our relations – rather than as polycultures – of diversity, interrelationality, and various forms of companionship with each other and the Earth.

61 Denise Ferreira da Silva, 'Reading the Dead: A Black Feminist Poethical Reading of Global Capital,' in *Otherwise Worlds: Against Settler Colonialism and Anti-Blackness*, ed. Tiffany L. King, Jenell Navarro, and Andrea Smith (Durham, NC: Duke University Press, 2020), 42.

62 Avery F. Gordon, *Ghostly Matters: Haunting and the Sociological Imagination* (Minneapolis: University of Minnesota Press, 2008), 3–5.

2 ATTRACTION

1 As a result of our disconformity from the social expectation that everyone inherently experiences sexual and romantic attraction, aces and aros face issues navigating the 'rules of attraction.' This can take many forms, such as when our behaviors are 'misread' as expressions of sexual or romantic attraction as well as when we sometimes miss sexual and romantic cues being signaled our way.

2 Steven Seidman, 'Theoretical perspectives,' in *Handbook of the New Sexuality Studies*, ed. Nancy Fischer and Chet Meeks (London: Routledge, 2007), 4–5.

3 Saskia Wieringa and Horacio Sívori, *The Sexual History of the Global South: Sexual Politics in Africa, Asia and Latin America* (London: Bloomsbury Publishing, 2013), 7.

4 Ibid.

5 Saskia Wieringa, *Heteronormativity, Passionate Aesthetics and Symbolic Subversion in Asia* (Chicago: Sussex Academic Press, 2015), 25.

6 Deborah A. Miranda, 'Extermination of the Joyas: Gendercide in Spanish California,' *GLQ: A Journal of Lesbian and Gay Studies* 16, no. 1–2 (2010): doi:10.1215/10642684-2009-022; H. Samy Alim et al., 'Language, Race, and the (Trans)Formation of Cisheteropatriarchy,' in *The Oxford Handbook of Language and Race*, ed. H. S. Alim, Angela Reyes, and Paul V. Kroskrity (New York: Oxford University Press, 2020), 293.

7 Wieringa, *Heteronormativity, Passionate Aesthetics and Symbolic Subversion in Asia,* 25.

8 Tim Lindsey and Helen Pausacker, *Crime and Punishment in Indonesia* (London: Routledge, 2020), 433.

9 Pete Sigal, *Infamous Desire: Male Homosexuality in Colonial Latin America* (Chicago: University of Chicago Press, 2003), 1.

10 H. Samy Alim et al., 'Language, Race, and the (Trans)Formation of Cisheteropatriarchy,' in *The Oxford Handbook of Language and Race,* ed. H. S. Alim, Angela Reyes, and Paul V. Kroskrity (New York: Oxford University Press, 2020), 293.

11 Patrisia Gonzales, *Red Medicine: Traditional Indigenous Rites of Birthing and Healing* (University of Arizona Press, 2012), 76–78.

12 Steven Seidman, 'Theoretical perspectives,' in *Handbook of the New Sexuality Studies,* ed. Nancy Fischer and Chet Meeks (London: Routledge, 2007), 4–5.

13 Sigal, *Infamous Desire,* 1.

14 Rahul Rao, *Out of Time: The Queer Politics of Postcoloniality* (New York: Oxford University Press, 2020), 7-9.

15 The gender binary is central to how attraction is labeled in Western terms. *Asexual* and *aromantic* are exceptions to this since they do not rely on gender for definition.

16 Francis Hutcheson, *An Essay on the Nature and Conduct of the Passions and Affections* (London: 1728), 68–72, https://books.google.com/books?id=tgE2AQAAMAAJ

17 Ibid., 81.

18 Ibid., 114.

19 Charles Fourier, *The Theory of the Four Movements,* ed. Gareth Stedman Jones and Ian Patterson (Cambridge: Cambridge University Press, 1996 [1808]), 15–17.

20 Ibid.

21 Wm. H. Channing, 'Translations from Fourier,' *The Phalanx or Journal of Social Science* 1, no. 2 (November 1843): 25–26, https://books.google.com/books?id=aoI2AQAAMAAJ

22 Albert Brisbane, *Theory of the Functions of the Human Passions: Followed by an Outline View of the Fundamental Principles of Fourier's Theory of Social Science* (New York: Miller, Orton, & Mulligan, 1856), 2.

23 Ibid., 117–118.

24 Ibid., 120.

25 Ibid., 121.

26 Ibid., 127.

27 Like a beautiful but chaotic web of threads that comprise a complex whole, the strands of attraction may mesh together and can frequently feel messy to be entwined within. For some people, certain strands may be absent, while for others they may be central. The various expressions of attraction may be merged, overlapped, or be in direct intimate contact with one another in which one cannot exist without the other, just as they may be understood as functioning more independently from one another.

28 This popular perception indicates that, in practice, many people already (implicitly and subconsciously) recognize that there are more than two genders. By being viewed as neither a 'real' man or woman, this places the 'effeminate' man and 'masculine' woman into a 'third' and 'fourth' (ostracized and negatively viewed) space (as many 'third gender' people and beyond were globally targeted in the wake of colonialism).

29 Steven Seidman, 'Theoretical perspectives,' in Handbook of the New Sexuality Studies, ed. Nancy Fischer and Chet Meeks (London: Routledge, 2007), 4–5.

30 Lillian Faderman, Surpassing the Love of Men: Romantic Friendship and Love Between Women from the Renaissance to the Present (New York: William Morrow and Company, 1981), 190.

31 Michelle Gibson, Lesbian Academic Couples (London: Routledge, 2012), 4.

32 Ibid.

33 William Brown, Talks on Psychotherapy (London: University of London Press, 1923), 59.

34 Public Documents of Massachusetts, Volume 5 (Canton, MA: Department of Public Welfare, 1940), 69.

35 Paul Bousfield, The Elements of Practical Psycho-analysis (London: Kegan Paul, Trench Trubner & Co. Ltd., 1922 [1920]), 81–82.

36 Arthur Tansley, The New Psychology and Its Relation to Life (London: George Allen and Unwin Ltd, 1910), 277.

37 Claire McLisky, '(En)gendering Faith?: Love, Marriage and the Evangelical Mission on the Settler Colonial Frontier,' in Studies in Settler

Colonialism: Politics, Identity and Culture, ed. Fiona Bateman and Lionel Pilkington (Basingstoke: Springer, 2011), 110–111.

38 Ana Catarina Carvalho and David L. Rodrigues, 'Sexuality, Sexual Behavior, and Relationships of Asexual Individuals: Differences Between Aromantic and Romantic Orientation,' *Archives of Sexual Behavior* 51 (2021): 2166, doi.org/10.1007/s10508-021-02187-2

39 Juliet Lapidos, 'What's Plato Got To Do With It?,' Slate Magazine, last modified September 26, 2010, https://slate.com/human-interest/2010/09/the-origins-of-the-term-platonic-friendship.html

40 Evelyn Abbott and Lewis Campbell, *The Life and Letters of Benjamin Jowett, M.A., Master of Balliol College, Oxford: Volume 2* (London: John Murray, 1897), 269–270.

41 William Rounseville Alger, *The Friendships of Women* (Boston: Roberts Brothers, 1868), 114–120.

42 D. W. Cummings, 'A Question of Conversion,' in *Improvement Era, Volume 17*, ed. Joseph F. Smith and Edward H. Anderson (Salt Lake City: General Board of the Young Men's Mutual Improvement Association, 1914), 27.

43 Emil Reich, *Plato as an Introduction to Modern Criticism of Life* (London: Chapman & Hall, Ltd., 1906), 258.

44 Gertrude Atherton, 'Platonic Friendship: V. By Gertrude Atherton,' in *The Lady's Realm: An Illustrated Monthly Magazine, Volume VII* (London: Hutchinson & Co., 1900), 591.

45 Abbott and Campbell, *The Life and Letters of Benjamin Jowett: Volume 2*, 269–270.

46 C. Heyland Fox, 'Platonic Friendship: VIII. By Mrs. C. Heyland Fox,' in *The Lady's Realm: An Illustrated Monthly Magazine, Volume VII* (London: Hutchinson & Co., 1900), 595.

47 E. R. Nash, 'Is Platonic Love A Normal Relation?,' in *Sexual Truths Versus Sexual Lies, Misconceptions, and Exaggerations*, ed. William J. Robinson (Hoboken, NJ: The American Biological Society, 1919), 304–306.

48 Arthur Belleville McCoid, *Husbands and Wives* (Chicago: St. Hubert Publishing Company, 1921), 144.

49 Richard Cleminson and Francisco V. García, ' "Quien Con Niños se Junta": Childhood and the Spectre of Homoerastia,' in *Los Invisibles: A History of Male Homosexuality in Spain, 1850–1940* (Cardiff: University of Wales Press, 2011), ebook.

50 Machiko Ishikawa, *Paradox and Representation: Silenced Voices in the Narratives of Nakagami Kenji* (Ithaca: Cornell University Press, 2020), 186–187.

51 Eve K. Sedgwick, *Between Men: English Literature and Male Homosocial Desire* (New York: Columbia University Press, 1992), 25–26.

52 Ishikawa, *Paradox and Representation: Silenced Voices in the Narratives of Nakagami Kenji*, 186–187.

53 William Rounseville Alger, 'Friendship between Women,' in *The Book of Friendship*, ed. Samuel McCord Crothers (New York: The Macmillan Company, 1910), 241–242.

54 Cummings, 'A Question of Conversion,' 27.

55 Stuart Eskrine, 'Platonic Friendship: V. By The Hon. Stuart Eskrine,' in *The Lady's Realm: An Illustrated Monthly Magazine, Volume VII* (London: Hutchinson & Co., 1900), 593.

56 Barbara J. Bank, *Contradictions in Women's Education: Traditionalism, Careerism, and Community at a Single-sex College* (New York: Teachers College Press, 2003), 110–111.

57 Abbott and Campbell, *The Life and Letters of Benjamin Jowett: Volume 2*, 269–270.

58 Heyland Fox, 'Platonic Friendship: VIII. By Mrs. C. Heyland Fox,' 595.

59 Sherronda J. Brown, 'Grieving Platonic Love in a Romance-driven World,' Scalawag Magazine, last modified April 7, 2022, https://scalawagmagazine.org/2022/04/grieving-platonic-love/

60 Leopold Loewenfeld, *On Conjugal Happiness: Experiences, Reflections and Advice of a Medical Man*, trans. Ronald E. S. Krohn (London: John Bale, Sons & Danielsson, Ltd., 1913), 165–166.

61 Oliver Phelps Brown, *The Complete Herbalist: Or, The People Their Own Physicians, by the Use of Nature's Remedies; Describing the Great Curative Properties Found in the Herbal Kingdom. A New and Plain System of Hygienic Principles, Together with Comprehensive Essays on Sexual Philosophy, Marriage, Divorce, &c* (Jersey City: Oliver Phelps Brown, 1874), 421.

62 Austin Kent, *Free Love: Or, a Philosophical Demonstration of the Non-exclusive Nature of Connubial Love, Also, a Review of the Exclusive Feature of the Fowlers, Adin Ballou, H. C. Wright and Andrew Jackson Davis on Marriage* (Hopkinton, NY: Austin Kent, 1857), 49.

63 Owls-Glass, *Rebel Brag and British Bluster: A Record of Unfulfilled Prophecies, Baffled Schemes, and Disappointed Hopes* (New York: The American News Company, 1865), 88.

64 Kent, *Free Love*, 52.

65 Bousfield, *The Elements of Practical Psycho-analysis*, 81–82.

66 Tansley, *The New Psychology and Its Relation to Life*, 277.

67 Johannes H. Hoop, *Character and the Unconscious: A Critical Exposition of the Psychology of Freud and of Jung*, trans. Elizabeth Trevelyan (London: Kegan Paul, Trench, Trubner & Co. Ltd., 1923), 92.

68 Tracy Clark-Flory, 'Tinder for Cuddling: This App Will Find You a Random Stranger to Spoon,' Salon, last modified September 19, 2014, https://www.salon.com/2014/09/18/tinder_for_cuddling_this_app_will_find_you_a_random_stranger_to_spoon/

69 Ibid.

70 Caitlin Dewey, 'I tried out Cuddlr, the "Tinder for cuddling," and all I got was severely creeped out,' *Washington Post*, last modified September 24, 2014, https://www.washingtonpost.com/news/the-intersect/wp/2014/09/24/i-tried-out-cuddlr-the-tinder-for-cuddling-and-all-i-got-was-severely-creeped-out/

71 Ibid.

72 Charlie Williams and Damon Brown, 'One Last Hug,' Medium, last modified March 16, 2015, https://medium.com/@charliewilliams/one-last-hug-ff07648f1900

73 Lauren Keating, 'New App Cuddlr is the Tinder for Cuddle Buddies,' Tech Times, last modified September 23, 2014, https://www.techtimes.com/articles/16311/20140923/new-app-cuddlr-tinder-cuddle-buddies.htm

74 Charlie Williams, 'It's Touch, Not Sex,' Medium, last modified September 24, 2014, https://medium.com/@charliewilliams/its-a-touch-not-sex-46a51b1dec7

75 Diana Raab, 'How Sensuality Can Heal,' *Psychology Today*, last modified February 17, 2021, https://www.psychologytoday.com/us/blog/the-empowerment-diary/202102/how-sensuality-can-heal

76 Williams and Brown, 'One Last Hug.'

77 Beatrice Hazlehurst, 'The Rise and Fall of Spoonr, an App That Connected Cuddlers,' *Paper*, last modified June 15, 2020, https://www.papermag.com/rise-and-fall-of-spoonr-2532238909.html

78 Michael Paramo, 'On Sensual Attraction: Yes, Sometimes People Do "Just Want to Cuddle",' *Medium*, last modified February 25, 2020, https://medium.com/@Michael_Paramo/on-sensual-attraction-yes-sometimes-people-do-just-want-to-cuddle-ef70fdb8d1f9

79 Lorca Jolene Sloan, 'Ace of (BDSM) clubs: Building asexual relationships through BDSM practice,' *Sexualities* 18, no. 5–6 (2015): 548, doi:10.1177/1363460714550907

80 Ibid., 553–555.

81 Bob O'Boyle, 'On Being Asexual and Kinky,' *AZE*, last modified April 1, 2018, https://azejournal.com/article/2018/4/1/bob-oboyle-on-being-asexual-and-kinky

82 Paranoidgynandroid, 'Questions Asked by Asexual and Questioning People,' Wayback Machine, last modified February 25, 2003, https://web.archive.org/web/20030225191733/http://www.asexuality.org/bigfaq.htm

83 Nicole Brinkley, 'Aesthetic Attraction and Being on the Asexual Spectrum,' *Archer Magazine*, last modified December 30, 2021, https://archermagazine.com.au/2017/04/aesthetic-attraction/

84 Theo Lieven, *Brand Gender: Increasing Brand Equity through Brand Personality* (Basingstoke: Springer, 2017), 152.

85 George Tucker, *Essays on Various Subjects of Taste, Morals, and National Policy* (Georgetown, DC: Joseph Milligan, 1822), 192.

86 Johann Georg Kohl, 'Scotland,' in *European Pamphlets, Volume 28* (Philadelphia: Carey and Hart, 1844), 54.

87 Knight Dunlap, *Personal Beauty and Racial Betterment* (St. Louis: C. V. Mosby Company, 1920), 20.

88 Ibid.

89 NAACP, 'Brown V. Board: The Significance of the "Doll Test,"' NAACP Legal Defense Fund, https://www.naacpldf.org/brown-vs-board/significance-doll-test/

90 Sharon-Ann Gopaul-McNicol, 'A Cross-Cultural Examination of Racial Identity and Racial Preference of Preschool Children in the West Indies,' *Journal of Cross-Cultural Psychology* 26, no. 2 (1995): doi:10.1177/0022022195262002

91 Adolfo Gamboa, 'My Waking Up,' *AZE*, last modified April 1, 2018, https://azejournal.com/article/2018/4/1/adolfo-gamboa-my-waking-up

92 Héctor Carrillo, *Pathways of Desire: The Sexual Migration of Mexican Gay Men* (Chicago: University of Chicago Press, 2018), 194–196.

93 Kevin J. Hsu, Ryan F. Lei, and Galen V. Bodenhausen, 'Racial preferences in sexual attraction among White heterosexual and gay men: Evidence from sexual arousal patterns and negative racial attitudes,' *Psychophysiology* 58, no. 11 (2021): doi:10.1111/psyp.13911

94 Michael Thai, Matthew J. Stainer, and Fiona K. Barlow, 'The "preference" paradox: Disclosing racial preferences in attraction is considered racist even by people who overtly claim it is not,' *Journal of Experimental Social Psychology* 83 (2019): doi:10.1016/j.jesp.2019.03.004

95 Livia Gershon, 'How Colonialism Shaped Body Shaming,' JSTOR Daily, last modified March 2, 2020, https://daily.jstor.org/how-colonialism-shaped-body-shaming/

96 Christopher E. Forth, 'Fat, Desire and Disgust in the Colonial Imagination,' *History Workshop Journal* 73 (Spring 2012): 215, doi:10.1093/hwj/dbr016

97 Henry T. Finck, *Primitive Love and Love-stories* (New York: Charles Scribner's Sons, 1899), 61.

98 Sabrina Strings, *Fearing the Black Body: The Racial Origins of Fat Phobia* (New York: NYU Press, 2019), 144–146.

99 Gershon, 'How Colonialism Shaped Body Shaming.'

100 Da'Shaun L. Harrison, *Belly of the Beast: The Politics of Anti-Fatness as Anti-Blackness* (Berkeley: North Atlantic Books, 2021), 12.

101 Rizvana Bradley and Denise Ferreira da Silva, 'Four Theses on Aesthetics,' E-flux, last modified September 2021, https://www.e-flux.com/journal/120/416146/four-theses-on-aesthetics/

102 Cindy Lamothe, 'Emotional Attraction: 16 FAQs, Signs and Tips,' Healthline, last modified October 14, 2019, https://www.healthline.com/health/emotional-attraction

103 Alanna Lauren Greco and Rachel Varina, 'Demiromantic,' *Cosmopolitan*, last modified October 27, 2021, https://www.cosmopolitan.com/sexopedia/a31094953/demiromantic-definition/

104 Selwyn Gould Langley, *Philogeny: The Science of Love and a Scientific System of Producing a Normal Race Through Love-Marriages* (Oakland: Shannon-Conmy Printing Company, 1915), 3–4.

105 Charles J. Whitby, *The Logic of Human Character* (London: Macmillan and Co., Limited, 1905), 97–99.

106 Albert Wilson, *Unfinished Man: A Scientific Analysis of the Psychopath or Human Degenerate* (London: Greening & Co., 1910), 162.

107 James T. Kunnanatt, 'Emotional intelligence: The new science of interpersonal effectiveness,' *Human Resource Development Quarterly* 15, no. 4 (2004): 490, doi:10.1002/hrdq.1117

108 Miguel Á. Sastre Castillo and Ignacio Danvila Del Valle, 'Is emotional intelligence the panacea for a better job performance? A study on low-skilled back office jobs,' *Employee Relations* 39, no. 5 (2017): doi:10.1108/er-11-2016-0216

109 Similar to colonial narratives concerning other forms of attraction, how each of us experiences emotional attraction does not have to be aligned with colonial value systems, even as these systems simultaneously have a powerful influence in shaping perceptions.

110 Lisa Wade, 'Doing Casual Sex: A Sexual Fields Approach to the Emotional Force of Hookup Culture,' *Social Problems* 68, no. 1 (2019): doi:10.1093/socpro/spz054

111 Jennifer S. Aubrey and Siobhan E. Smith, 'Development and Validation of the Endorsement of the Hookup Culture Index,' *Journal of Sex Research* 50, no. 5 (2011): doi:10.1080/00224499.2011.637246

112 Reilly Kincaid, Christie Sennott, and Brian C. Kelly, 'Doing and Redoing Emphasized Femininity: How Women Use Emotion Work to Manage Competing Expectations in College Hookup Culture,' *Sex Roles* 86, no. 5–6 (2022): doi:10.1007/s11199-022-01275-4

113 LGBTQ Center, 'Asexuality, Attraction, and Romantic Orientation,' University of North Carolina, Chapel Hill, last modified July 1, 2021, https://lgbtq.unc.edu/resources/exploring-identities/asexuality-attraction-and-romantic-orientation

114 Mere Abrams, '37 Terms That Describe Different Types of Attraction,' Healthline, last modified December 23, 2021, https://www.healthline.com/health/types-of-attraction

115 Terence T. Gorski, *Getting Love Right: Learning the Choices of Healthy Intimacy* (New York: Simon & Schuster, 1993), 231.

116 August Bebel, *Woman and Socialism* (New York City: Socialist Literature Company, 1910), 105.

117 Antony Koch, *A Handbook of Moral Theology Volume II: Sin and the Means of Grace*, ed. Arthur Preuss (St. Louis: B. Herder Book Company, 1919), 204.

118 Ayala Malach Pines, *Couple Burnout: Causes and Cures* (London: Routledge, 1996), 214.

119 LiveJournal, 'Stoked on Sapiosexuality,' LiveJournal, last modified March 15, 2002, https://wolfieboy.livejournal.com/2262.html

120 Ibid.

121 Neda Ulaby, 'Sapiosexual Seeks Same: A New Lexicon Enters Online Dating Mainstream,' NPR.org, last modified December 4, 2014, https://www.npr.org/sections/alltechconsidered/2014/12/04/368441691/sapiosexual-seeks-same-a-new-lexicon-enters-online-dating-mainstream

122 Steven Blum, 'People Who Only Want to Fuck Smart People Created Their Own "Sexual Orientation",' VICE, last modified December 6, 2016, https://www.vice.com/en/article/43gd5p/sapiosexuals-people-who-only-have-sex-with-smart-people

123 OkCupid, 'Gender and Orientation on OkCupid,' OkCupid Dating App Help Page, accessed February 20, 2022, https://help.okcupid.com/article/208-gender-and-orientation-on-okcupid

124 Merriam-Webster, 'What Does "Sapiosexual" Mean?,' accessed February 20, 2022, https://www.merriam-webster.com/words-at-play/the-hearts-wisdom-what-does-sapiosexual-mean

125 WebMD Editorial Contributors, 'Sapiosexual: What It Means,' WebMD, last modified November 21, 2020, https://www.webmd.com/sex/sapiosexual-what-it-means

126 Carina Hsieh and Frank Kobola, '6 People on What It's Like to Be Sapiosexual,' *Cosmopolitan*, last modified July 18, 2018, https://www.cosmopolitan.com/sex-love/a9535309/sapiosexual-definition-facts/

127 Paula Butler, *Colonial Extractions: Race and Canadian Mining in Contemporary Africa* (Toronto: University of Toronto Press, 2015), 188.

128 Chrystos, 'Chrystos speaks at Creating Change 2011,' National LGBTQ Task Force, YouTube, last modified February 24, 2011, https://www.youtube.com/watch?v=vZcLj-caeOE&ab_channel=NationalLGBTQTaskForce

3 The Cyberspatial Emergence of Asexual Identity

1 'Committed, Loving, Asexual Relationships,' Usenet via Google Groups, last modified December 27, 1990, https://groups.google.com/g/soc.couples/c/LOhlKp6MS_o/m/oYaYexRpl2wJ

2 Ibid.

3 Ibid.

4 Ibid.

5 Ibid.

6 As a side note, I discovered a response to an unrelated soc.couples discussion topic titled 'wow!' in 1994 that stated: "Hell, if you're asexual and you've found a partner which this works with, I'm glad for you too!" The user was critiquing the original poster, who diminished non-monogamous or 'open relationships.'

7 'Committed, Loving, Asexual Relationships,' Usenet via Google Groups, last modified December 27, 1990, https://groups.google.com/g/soc.couples/c/LOhlKp6MS_o/m/oYaYexRpl2wJ

8 Ibid.

9 'Committed, Loving, Asexual Relationships,' Usenet via Google Groups, last modified December 30, 1990, https://groups.google.com/g/soc.couples/c/IVJNrMR_In4/m/lzs6OMdODxcJ

10 'I'm Asexual!,' Usenet via Google Groups, last modified May 22, 1993, https://groups.google.com/g/soc.bi/c/soz_lwRznkg/m/3YAym_YrYf4J

11 Ibid.

12 Ibid.

13 'Sexual Preferences and Stuff..,' Usenet via Google Groups, last modified June 4, 1993, https://groups.google.com/g/soc.bi/c/YSp5YRl6yPo/m/uAyWltjd4FEJ

14 Ibid.

15 Catherine Clifford, 'On Running and Asexual Embodiment,' *AZE*, last modified June 2019, https://azejournal.com/article/2019/6/3/on-running-and-asexual-embodiment

16 Alba, 'The Asexual Agenda,' *AZE*, last modified July 2018, https://azejournal.com/article/2018/6/29/the-asexual-agenda

17 WebMD Editorial Contributors, 'What Does Aromantic Mean?,' WebMD, last modified June 27, 2021, https://www.webmd.com/sex/what-does-aromantic-mean

18 Esther D. Rothblum, Kyra Heimann, and Kylie Carpenter, 'The lives of asexual individuals outside of sexual and romantic relationships: education, occupation, religion and community,' *Psychology & Sexuality* 10, no. 1 (2018): 91, doi:10.1080/19419899.2018.1552186

19 Alex Henderson, 'Asexual Positivity in a Game About Sexy Demons,' *AZE*, last modified July 2018, https://azejournal.com/article/2018/6/29/asexual-positivity-in-a-game-about-sexy-demons

20 Jessica Vazquez, 'Coming Out Twice: On Being Gay and Asexual in a World Without Representation,' Autostraddle, last modified April 17, 2021, https://www.autostraddle.com/coming-out-twice-on-being-gay-and-asexual-in-a-world-without-representation/

21 Zoe O'Reilly, '19x52: My Life As an Amoeba,' Wayback Machine (originally posted to AZStarNet.com), last modified May 30, 1997, https://web.archive.org/web/20030210212218/dispatches.azstarnet.com/zoe/amoeba.htm

22 Ibid.

23 Ibid.

24 Lwazi Lushaba, 'Decolonial Thought Lecture 4,' YouTube, last modified February 2, 2017, https://www.youtube.com/watch?v=3ugWXYCfeUQ

25 Zoe O'Reilly, '19x52: My Life As an Amoeba,' Wayback Machine, last modified May 30, 1997, https://web.archive.org/web/20030210212218/dispatches.azstarnet.com/zoe/amoeba.htm

26 Comments to Zoe O'Reilly, '19x52: My Life As an Amoeba,' Wayback Machine, last modified May 30, 1997, https://web.archive.org/web/20030305150007/http://dispatches.azstarnet.com/zoe/amoeba2.htm

27 Ibid.

28 Ibid.

29 Ibid.

30 Asexual Visibility and Education Network, 'AVEN Discussion Forum,' Wayback Machine, last modified August 7, 2002, https://web.archive.org/web/20020807202545/www.asexuality.org/discussion/

31 Asexual Visibility and Education Network, 'FAQ,' Wayback Machine, last modified June 1, 2002, https://web.archive.org/web/20020601134559/asexuality.org/

32 Paranoidgynandroid, 'Questions Asked by Asexual and Questioning People,' Wayback Machine, last modified February 25, 2003, https://web.archive.org/web/20030225191733/http://www.asexuality.org/bigfaq.htm

33 Ibid.

34 Ibid.

35 Ibid.

4 Victorian Desirelessness and (Un)civilized Desires

1 William A. Hammond, *Sexual Impotence in the Male and Female* (New York: Birmingham & Co, 1887 [1884]), 12–14.

2 Bonnie E. Blustein, *Preserve Your Love for Science: Life of William A. Hammond, American Neurologist* (Cambridge; New York: Cambridge University Press, 2002), 7.

3 Ibid., 54.

4 Hammond, *Sexual Impotence in the Male and Female*, 12.

5 Ibid.

6 Blustein, *Preserve Your Love for Science*, 196.

7 Peter Cryle and Alison Moore, *Frigidity: An Intellectual History* (Basingstoke: Springer, 2011), 92–93.

8 Hammond, *Sexual Impotence in the Male and Female*, 15. Hammond makes this assertion under the heading of 'Acquired Absence of Desire,' which is discussed following his section entitled 'Original Absence of All Sexual Desire' in the text. The passage is used here to demonstrate his belief in the naturalness of sexual desire and his perception of 'civilization.'

9 Steven Seidman, 'Theoretical Perspectives,' in *Introducing the New Sexuality Studies: Original Essays and Interviews*, ed. Steven Seidman, Nancy Fischer, and Chet Meeks (Abingdon; New York: Routledge, 2006), 4.

10 Ela Przybylo and Danielle Cooper, 'Asexual Resonances,' *GLQ: A Journal of Lesbian and Gay Studies* 20, no. 3 (2014): 298–299, doi:10.1215/10642684-2422683

11 Patti Duncan, 'history of disease,' in *Q & A: Queer in Asian America*, ed. David L. Eng and Alica Y. Hom (Philadelphia: Temple University Press, 1998), 164.

12 Hammond, *Sexual Impotence in the Male and Female*, 12–13.

13 Michel Foucault, *The History of Sexuality Volume 1: An Introduction* (New York: Pantheon Books, 1990 [1976]), 33.

14 Ibid., 45–46.

15 Richard Krafft-Ebing, *Psychopathia Sexualis* (London: F.A. Davis Company, 1894 [1886]), 42–47.

16 Foucault, *The History of Sexuality Volume 1*, 64.

17 Hammond, *Sexual Impotence in the Male and Female*, 10.

18 Cryle and Moore, *Frigidity*, 187.

19 Peter Boag, *Re-Dressing America's Frontier Past* (Oakland: University of California Press, 2012), 4–5.

20 Vera S. Maass, *Facing the Complexities of Women's Sexual Desire* (Berlin: Springer Science & Business Media, 2006), 6.

21 Boag, *Re-Dressing America's Frontier Past*, 5.

22 Mr. W is assumed here to be a Euro-immigrant or white, based on Hammond's description of the man. If any of Hammond's patients were non-European, it is reasonable to assume that Hammond would have noted this, especially given his unabashed racism that is mentioned later in the chapter.

23 Gail Bederman, *Manliness and Civilization: A Cultural History of Gender and Race in the United States, 1880–1917* (Chicago: University of Chicago Press, 1995), 48.

24 Louise Hardwick, *New Approaches to Crime in French Literature, Culture and Film* (Bern: Peter Lang AG, 2009), 29.

25 Bederman, *Manliness and Civilization*, 48.

26 Ibid.

27 Hammond, *Sexual Impotence in the Male and Female*, 14.

28 Elizabeth Jameson, 'Bringing It All Back Home: Rethinking the History of Women and the Nineteenth-Century West,' in *A Companion to the American West*, ed. William Deverell (Hoboken: John Wiley & Sons, 2008), 191. Jameson discusses that "efforts to control intimate practices of marriage, sexuality, reproduction, and inheritance illuminate social power throughout the West, the stakes for all the players, and the limits of women's historical agency." Through portraying the subordination

of women within these intimate practices, Jameson illustrates the unequal agency that was expected to be socially afforded to men through marriage.

29 Bederman, *Manliness and Civilization*, 48.

30 Arthur W. Hunt, *The Vanishing Word: The Veneration of Visual Imagery in the Postmodern World* (Eugene: Wipf and Stock Publishers, 2013), 116–117.

31 Hammond, *Sexual Impotence in the Male and Female*, 12–13.

32 Ibid.

33 Ibid., 13.

34 Bederman, *Manliness and Civilization*, 82.

35 Ibid., 83.

36 George C. Denniston and Marilyn F. Milos, *Sexual Mutilations: A Human Tragedy* (Berlin: Springer Science & Business Media, 2013), 23.

37 Hammond, *Sexual Impotence in the Male and Female*, 14.

38 Ibid., 281–282.

39 Bederman, *Manliness and Civilization*, 11.

40 Maass, *Facing the Complexities of Women's Sexual Desire*, 6.

41 Kara Platoni, 'The Sex Scholar,' *Stanford Magazine*, last modified April 2010, https://alumni.stanford.edu/get/page/magazine/article/?article_id=29954

42 Karen Lystra, *Searching the Heart: Women, Men, and Romantic Love in Nineteenth-Century America* (New York: Oxford University Press, 1992), 59.

43 Hammond, *Sexual Impotence in the Male and Female*, 282.

44 Victoria C. Woodhull, *A Speech on the Principles of Social Freedom* (New York: Claflin and Company, 1872), 16.

45 Helen L. Horowitz, 'Victoria Woodhull, Anthony Comstock, and Conflict over Sex in the United States in the 1870s,' *Journal of American History* 87, no. 2 (2000): 414, doi:10.2307/2568758

46 Jill E. Hasday, 'Contest and Consent: A Legal History of Marital Rape,' *California Law Review* 88, no. 5 (2000): 1392, doi:10.2307/3481263

47 Hammond, *Sexual Impotence in the Male and Female*, 282.

48 Jennifer C. Kelsey, *Changing The Rules: Women and Victorian Marriage* (Troubador Publishing, 2016), 207.

49 Hammond, *Sexual Impotence in the Male and Female*, 282–283.

50 Ibid., 282.

51 Eunjung Kim, 'On the Racialization of Asexuality,' in *Asexualities: Feminist and Queer Perspectives*, ed. Karli J. Cerankowski and Megan Milks (London: Routledge, 2014), 485.

52 Kelsey, *Changing The Rules*, 207. Just as it was deemed to be a conjugal duty of wives to satisfy the sexual advances of their husbands by way of submission, it was also understood as a marital duty of wives to accept 'each pregnancy as it arose,' which was reinforced in popular advice-literature at the time. It is unknown if or how this may have influenced Mrs. C's desire to have a child.

53 Hammond, *Sexual Impotence in the Male and Female*, 283.

54 Ibid., 282.

55 Ibid., 14.

56 Ibid., 15.

57 Ibid., 283.

58 Ibid.

59 4 *Re-Dressing America's Frontier Past*, 6.

60 Foucault, *The History of Sexuality Volume 1*, 43.

61 Graham Robb, *Strangers: Homosexual Love in the Nineteenth Century* (New York: W. W. Norton & Company, 2005), 47–48.

62 Hammond, *Sexual Impotence in the Male and Female*, 278.

63 Blustein, *Preserve Your Love for Science*, 192.

64 Foucault, *The History of Sexuality Volume 1*, 114; 146–147.

65 Timothy L. Carens, *Outlandish English Subjects in the Victorian Domestic Novel* (Palgrave Macmillan, 2005), 28.

66 Hammond, *Sexual Impotence in the Male and Female*, 130.

67 Blustein, *Preserve Your Love for Science*, 192.

68 Ianna H. Owen, 'On the Racialization of Asexuality,' in *Asexualities: Feminist and Queer Perspectives*, ed. Karli J. Cerankowski and Megan Milks (London: Routledge, 2014), 256.

69 Hammond, *Sexual Impotence in the Male and Female*, 278.

70 Ibid., 31.

71 Ibid., 284. Hammond recommended to Mrs. O that "there appears to be no indication for treatment for no part of the generative apparatus seems to be at fault."

72 Vanessa Baird, *The No-nonsense Guide to Sexual Diversity* (Oxford: New Internationalist, 2007), 107.

73 Owen, 'On the Racialization of Asexuality,' 262.

74 Joan Perkin, *Victorian Women* (New York: NYU Press, 1995), 68.

75 Foucault, *The History of Sexuality Volume 1*, 36–37.

76 Hammond seems to be referring here to a person being born 'defect-ive,' although this is not clarified.

77 Hammond, *Sexual Impotence in the Male and Female*, 284.

78 Henry L. Minton, *Departing from Deviance: A History of Homosexual Rights and Emancipatory Science in America* (Chicago: University of Chicago Press, 2010), 15.

79 Gardner W. Allen, 'The Etiology and Pathology of Impotence,' *Journal of Cutaneous and Genito-urinary Diseases* 11 (1893): 443.

80 Thank you to Dr. Susie Woo for editing several early drafts of this essay while I was a graduate student at California State University, Fullerton.

5 On Love and the (A)romantic

1 Jacques Van Lankveld et al., 'The associations of intimacy and sexu-ality in daily life,' *Journal of Social and Personal Relationships* 35, no. 4 (2018): 557, doi:10.1177/0265407517743076. This conclusion was asserted on the basis of other studies.

2 Chalandra M. Bryant and Rand D. Conger, 'An Intergenerational Model of Romantic Relationship Development,' in *Stability and Change in Relationships*, ed. Anita L. Vangelisti, Harry T. Reis, and Mary A. Fitzpatrick (Cambridge: Cambridge University Press, 2002), 57. This conclusion was asserted on the basis of other studies.

3 Alexandra Cunningham et al., 'The Effects of a Romantic Relation-ship Treatment Option for Adults With Autism Spectrum Disorder,' *Counseling Outcome Research and Evaluation* 7, no. 2 (2016): 99, doi: 10.1177/2150137816668561

4 Wendy Wang and Kim Parker, 'Record Share of Americans Have Never Married,' Pew Research Center's Social & Demographic Trends Project, last modified August 27, 2020, https://www.pewre-search.org/social-trends/2014/09/24/record-share-of-americans-have-never-married/

5 Feargus O'Sullivan, 'Where Europeans Are Most Likely to Be Single vs. Married,' Bloomberg, last modified October 14, 2015, https://www.bloomberg.com/news/articles/2015-10-14/maps-of-where-europeans-are-more-likely-to-be-single-instead-of-married

6 Katarzyna Adamczyk, 'An Investigation of Loneliness and Perceived Social Support Among Single and Partnered Young Adults,' *Current Psychology* 35, no. 4 (2015): 674, doi:10.1007/s12144-015-9337-7

7 Colin Campbell, '"All You Need Is Love": From Romance to Romanticism: The Beatles, Romantic Love, and Cultural Change,' in *Romantic Love*, ed. Yolanda Van Ede (Münster: LIT Verlag Münster, 2007), 112–113

8 'The History of Romance,' National Women's History Museum, last modified February 13, 2017, https://www.womenshistory.org/articles/history-romance

9 Van Ede, *Romantic Love*, 11.

10 Campbell, ' "All You Need Is Love": From Romance to Romanticism,' 112–113.

11 Eliza Haywood, *Love in Excess – Second Edition*, ed. David Oakleaf (Ontario: Broadview Press, 2000), 11–12.

12 Jeremy Black, *Culture in Eighteenth-Century England: A Subject for Taste* (London: A&C Black, 2007), 154.

13 Campbell, ' "All You Need Is Love": From Romance to Romanticism,' 112–113.

14 Ibid. Campbell argues that romantic love in this context still remains controversial, suggesting that critiques of the idea that romantic love should function as the primary basis of a relationship still pervade in societal attitudes today through common advice given to potential couples that they should also "pay equal weight to more sober and utilitarian considerations."

15 Kari E. Lokke, *Tracing Women's Romanticism: Gender, History, and Transcendence* (London: Routledge, 2004), 68.

16 Mary Shelley, *Valperga: Or, The Life and Adventures of Castruccio, Prince of Lucca Volume 2* (London: G. and W. B. Whittaker, 1823), 87–88.

17 Lokke, *Tracing Women's Romanticism*, 68.

18 Ibid.

19 'Plato: The Timaeus,' Internet Encyclopedia of Philosophy, accessed March 13, 2022, https://iep.utm.edu/timaeus/

20 Juliet Lapidos, 'What's Plato Got To Do With It?,' Slate Magazine, last modified September 26, 2010, https://slate.com/human-interest/2010/09/the-origins-of-the-term-platonic-friendship.html

21 A. F. Scott, *Current Literary Terms: A Concise Dictionary of their Origin and Use* (Basingstoke: Macmillan, 1965), 221–222.

22 'Why We Keep Things "Platonic",' Merriam-Webster, last modified February 22, 2021, https://www.merriam-webster.com/words-at-play/platonic-plato-love-origin-history

23 Ibid.

24 Ibid.

25 Samuel Richardson, *Pamela; or, Virtue Rewarded Volume IV* (London: Messrs Rivington & Osborn, 1801 [1740]), 200.

26 Harriet Maria Gordon Smythies, *A Warning to Wives: Or, The Platonic Lover: A Novel* (London: T. C. Newby, 1848), 175–176.

27 *A Lecture on Love: In Three Parts* (Stranraer: D. Duncan, 1816), 42–43.

28 Henry T. Finck, *Romantic Love and Personal Beauty: Their Development, Causal Relations, Historic and National Peculiarities Volume II* (London: Macmillan and Co., 1887), 128.

29 Finck, *Romantic Love and Personal Beauty*, 128.

30 Ibid., 129.

31 Plato, *Symposium*, ed. Christopher Gill (New York: Penguin, 2003), 54–55.

32 Finck, *Romantic Love and Personal Beauty*, 129.

33 Ibid., 130.

34 Juliet Lapidos, 'What's Plato Got To Do With It?,' Slate Magazine, last modified September 26, 2010, https://slate.com/human-interest/2010/09/the-origins-of-the-term-platonic-friendship.html

35 Finck, *Romantic Love and Personal Beauty*, 128.

36 Finck, *Primitive Love and Love-stories*, 774.

37 'Plato, Timaeus, Section 90e,' Perseus Digital Library, accessed March 6, 2022, http://data.perseus.org/citations/urn:cts:greekLit:tlg0059.tlg031.perseus-eng1:90e

38 'Plato, Timaeus, Section 91a,' Perseus Digital Library, accessed March 6, 2022, http://data.perseus.org/citations/urn:cts:greekLit:tlg0059.tlg031.perseus-eng1:91a

39 'Plato, Timaeus, Section 91d,' Perseus Digital Library, accessed March 6, 2022, http://data.perseus.org/citations/urn:cts:greekLit:tlg0059.tlg031.perseus-eng1:91d

40 'Plato, Timaeus, Section 92b,' Perseus Digital Library, accessed March 6, 2022, http://data.perseus.org/citations/urn:cts:greekLit: tlg0059.tlg031.perseus-eng1:92b

41 'Plato, Laws, Book 6, Page 781,' Perseus Digital Library, accessed March 6, 2022, http://data.perseus.org/citations/urn:cts:greekLit: tlg0059.tlg034.perseus-eng1:6.781

42 Finck, *Primitive Love and Love-stories*, 773.

43 Plato, *Symposium*, xxii.

44 Finck, *Primitive Love and Love-stories*, 16–17.

45 Ibid., 773.

46 Ibid., 169.

47 Ibid., 2.

48 Quoted from Pramod K. Nayar, *Days of the Raj: Life and Leisure in British India* (New Delhi: Penguin Books India, 2009), 211.

49 J. C. Beltrami, *A Pilgrimage in Europe and America: Leading to the Discovery of the Sources of the Mississippi and Bloody River: with a Description of the Whole Course of the Former and of the Ohio Volume II* (London: Hunt and Clarke, 1828), 245.

50 Finck, *Primitive Love and Love-stories*, 169.

51 Ibid.

52 Ibid., 2.

53 Ibid., 17.

54 Fotis Kapetopoulos, 'When Did I Become "white"?,' Neos Kosmos, last modified May 7, 2021, https://neoskosmos.com/en/2016/10/31/ dialogue/opinion/when-did-greeks-become-white/

55 Finck, *Primitive Love and Love-stories*, 774. The stereotype of the more inherently misogynistic 'Greek man' that Finck is clearly referencing still pervades today. See: Kapetopoulos (2021).

56 Ibid., 771.

57 A term used to refer to cultural history.

58 Ibid., 781.

59 Ibid., 17.

60 Ibid., 17. As Finck stated, "Morgan found that the most advanced of American Indians, the Iroquois, had no capacity for love."

61 Lewis H. Morgan, *Systems of Consanguinity and Affinity of the Human Family* (Washington D. C.: Smithsonian Institution, 1871), 207.

62 Sir John Lubbock, *The Origin of Civilisation and the Primitive Condition of Man: Mental and Social Conditions of Savages* (London: Longmans, Green, and Co., 1870), 58.

63 William D. Whitney and Benjamin E. Smith, eds., *The Century Dictionary and Cyclopedia Volume 1* (New York: The Century Co., 1897), 701.

64 Bert Bender, *Evolution and 'the Sex Problem': American Narratives During the Eclipse of Darwinism* (Kent, OH: Kent State University Press, 2004), 39.

65 Paulette Richards, *Terry McMillan: A Critical Companion* (Santa Barbara: Greenwood Publishing Group, 1999), 43.

66 Clevis Headley, 'Philosophy as Excited Delirium and the Credibility Deficit of the Black Male,' in *Black Men from Behind the Veil: Ontological Interrogations*, ed. George Yancy (Lanham: Rowman & Littlefield, 2021), 35.

67 Geraldine Brown and Paul Grant, 'Hear Our Voices: We're More than the Hyper-masculine Label-Reasonings of Black Men Participating in a Faith-Based Prison Program,' in *New Perspectives on Prison Masculinities*, ed. Matthew Maycock and Kate Hunt (Basingstoke: Springer, 2018), 165.

68 Adaljiza Sosa Riddell, 'Chicanas and El Movimiento,' in *Chicana Feminist Thought: The Basic Historical Writings*, ed. Mario T. Garcia and Alma M. Garcia (London: Routledge, 1997), 92–94.

69 Finck's aforementioned *Primitive Love and Love-stories* is just one of many textbook examples of the result of this superiority complex actualized in book form. In his section 'How American Indians Love,' Finck compiled an array of colonial sources to allegedly support the idea that the masculine subjugation of women and the inability to love were intrinsic to the "savage," "barbarous," and "semi-civilized" Indigenous peoples of Turtle Island and Abya Yala.

70 Ibid.

71 Robin Goodwin, *Personal Relationships Across Cultures* (London: Routledge, 1999), 61–62.

72 Conrad L. Kanagy and Donald B. Kraybill, *The Riddles of Human Society* (Thousand Oaks: SAGE, 1999), 35.

73 Ibid.

74 Ibid.

75 Finck, *Romantic Love and Personal Beauty*, 201.

76 Tuula Gordon, *Single Women: On the Margins?* (London: Macmillan International Higher Education, 2016), 129. In addition to economic concerns, social attitudes have long perpetuated a negative stigma around single women. While a single man is more likely to be viewed with less negative stigma, reflecting notions of 'the playboy' or 'bachelor,' tropes that themselves are predicated on alleged sexual prowess over women, tropes of single women are either that she is sexually 'loose' or an 'old maid' – a stereotype that Gordon argues frames single women as "lacking something, being incomplete, [or] deviating from the norm and the normal."

77 Lokke, *Tracing Women's Romanticism*, 68.

78 David M. Newman and Elizabeth Grauerholz, *Sociology of Families* (Thousand Oaks: SAGE, 2002), 205–206.

79 Kenneth L. Dion and Karen K. Dion, 'Romantic Love: Individual and Cultural Perspectives,' in *The Psychology of Love*, ed. Robert J. Sternberg and Michael L. Barnes (New Haven: Yale University Press, 1988), 286. The authors record that in more highly individualistic societies such as the United States, even romantic love can sometimes be interpreted as a stumbling block for the instant fulfillment of individualistic desires: "Americans confront several problems in reconciling their sense of expressive individualism and self with the ideals of a love relationship [. . .] the spirit of American individualism makes it difficult for either partner in the relationship to justify sacrificing or giving to the other more than one is receiving. [. . .] This perhaps suggests that even romance cannot always 'keep up' with the pursuit of individualist desires."

80 Lokke, *Tracing Women's Romanticism*, 68.

81 Robert M. Polhemus, *Erotic Faith: Being in Love from Jane Austen to D. H. Lawrence* (Chicago: University of Chicago Press, 1995), 62–63.

82 Rizvana Bradley and Denise Ferreira da Silva, 'Four Theses on Aesthetics,' E-flux, last modified September 2021, https://www.e-flux.com/journal/120/416146/four-theses-on-aesthetics/

83 Hortense Spillers, 'Shades of Intimacy: Women in the Time of Revolution,' YouTube, February 21, 2017, https://www.youtube.com/watch?v=KPa7KhbuEJo&t

84 More-than-human refers to all of the life forms on Earth that coexist along with the human world.

85　It is not surprising then that the individualistic framework might paint this form of love as antithetical to 'freedom.'

86　Chela Sandoval, *Methodology of the Oppressed* (Minneapolis: University of Minnesota Press, 2000), 141.

87　Ibid., 'Introduction.'

88　Jesica Siham Fernández, *Decolonial Enactments in Community Psychology*, ed. Shahnaaz Suffla et al. (Cham: Springer Nature Switzerland, 2021), 46.

89　Last Moyo, *The Decolonial Turn in Media Studies in Africa and the Global South* (Cham: Springer Nature Switzerland, 2020), 74.

90　Yomaira C. Figueroa, 'Reparation as transformation: Radical literary (re)imaginings of futurities through decolonial love,' *Decolonization: Indigeneity, Education & Society* 4, no. 1 (2015): 43, https://jps.library.utoronto.ca/index.php/des/article/view/22151

91　Laura Harjo, *Spiral to the Stars: Mvskoke Tools of Futurity* (Tucson: University of Arizona Press, 2019), 73.

92　The idea that legitimate relationships should be based on anything other than the mutual expression of romantic love is still commonly rejected in the West. Perhaps then it is of no surprise that an identity like *aromantic* would sprout in the West, as in other contexts the issue of romantic love may not necessarily be viewed as a necessary element in one's life or relationships to the same extent. Therefore, to develop such a concept as *aromanticism*, defined as the absence or lack of romantic attraction, may not be as urgent in contexts where romance itself was never understood as essential to life, love, and fulfillment.

93　UnYoung, 'Care, Uncoupled,' *AZE*, last modified May 3, 2021, https://azejournal.com/article/2021/4/24/care-uncoupled

6 Notes from the Agender Refuge

1　Source: Oxford Languages.

2　'What Does It Mean to Be Agender?,' Them, last modified August 7, 2018, https://www.them.us/story/inqueery-agender

3　Sian Ferguson, 'What Does It Mean to Be Agender?,' Healthline, last modified January 20, 2021, https://www.healthline.com/health/agender

4 If gender functioned in a less restrictive manner, there may have been less urgency to deconstruct it.

5 Heidi Samuelson, 'Pronouns Are for Other People,' *AZE*, last modified November 14, 2018, https://azejournal.com/article/2018/11/8/pronouns-are-for-other-people

6 Shei, 'Thoughts on Being a Fem Agender: And Never Feeling Queer Enough,' *AZE*, last modified November 14, 2018, https://azejournal.com/article/2018/11/8/thoughts-on-being-a-fem-agender-and-never-feeling-queer-enough

7 David A. Binder and Riane Eisler, 'October Term, 1970: No. 5175: Amicus Curiae Brief,' in *Records and Briefs of the United States Supreme Court* (Cambridge, MA: Harvard Law School Library, 1970), 23–26, https://books.google.com/books?id=Jc2O9j9TBMEC

8 Gerard J. M. van den Aardweg, 'Parents of Homosexuals – Not Guilty? Interpretation of Childhood Psychological Data,' *American Journal of Psychotherapy* 38, no. 1 (January 1964): 188.

9 Merl Storr, 'Transformations: Subjects, Categories and Cures in Krafft-Ebing's Sexology,' in *Sexology in Culture: Labelling Bodies and Desires*, ed. Lucy Bland and Laura Doan (Chicago: University of Chicago Press, 1998), 14.

10 Richard Krafft-Ebing, *Psychopathia Sexualis* (London: F.A. Davis Company, 1894 [1886]), 28.

11 Annie L. Mearkle, 'The Woman Who Wants To Be A Man,' in *The Midland Monthly Volume 9*, ed. Johnson Brigham (Des Moines: Conaway & Shaw, 1898), 173–177.

12 Rutherford H. Towner, *The Philosophy of Civilization Volume 2* (New York & London: G. P. Putnam's Sons, 1923), 78–79.

13 Deborah A. Miranda, 'Extermination of the Joyas: Gendercide in Spanish California,' *GLQ: A Journal of Lesbian and Gay Studies* 16, no. 1–2 (2010): 253–284, doi:10.1215/10642684-2009-022

14 Scott L. Morgensen, *Spaces Between Us: Queer Settler Colonialism and Indigenous Decolonization* (Minneapolis: University of Minnesota Press, 2011), 37.

15 Yvette Abrahams, 'Precolonial Societies on Gender and Sexuality: A Hindu, Muslim and Indigenous Peoples' Perspective,' Muslims For Progressive Values, last modified October 12, 2019, https://www.youtube.com/watch?v=lvQlNIQYbwc

16 Wade Blevins, 'Gender in Pre-Columbian Cultures and Native Communities Today,' Gilcrease Museum, last modified November 1, 2018, https://www.youtube.com/watch?v=rlnWNJT5Tz0&ab_channel= GilcreaseMuseum

17 Chrystos, 'Chrystos speaks at Creating Change 2011,' National LGBTQ Task Force, YouTube, last modified February 24, 2011, https://www.youtube.com/watch?v=vZcLj-caeOE&ab_ channel=NationalLGBTQTaskForce

18 Laura E. Perez, 'Spirit Glyphs: Reimagining Art and Artist in the Work of Chicana Tlamatinime,' *MFS Modern Fiction Studies* 44, no. 1 (1998): 37, doi:10.1353/mfs.1998.0009

Conclusion

1 Theresa A. Yugar, Juan A. Tavárez, and Alan A. Barrera, 'The Enlightened West and the Origins of Climate Change,' *Journal of Feminist Studies in Religion* 33, no. 2 (Fall 2017): 168, doi:10.2979/ jfemistudreli.33.2.18

2 Elewani Ramugondo, 'Decolonialisation in the context of UCT's Vision for 2030,' University of Cape Town South Africa, YouTube, September 22, 2020, https://www.youtube.com/watch?v=NFIN hvywoNM&ab_channel=UniversityofCapeTownSouthAfrica

3 James Y. Henderson, 'Ayukpachi: Empowering Aboriginal Thought,' in *Protecting Indigenous Knowledge and Heritage: A Global Challenge*, ed. Marie A. Battiste (Vancouver: UBC Press, 2000), 248–249.

4 Lisa Grayshield, Marilyn Begay, and Laura L. Lena, 'IWOK Epistemology in Counseling Praxis,' in *Indigenous Ways of Knowing in Counseling: Theory, Research, and Practice*, ed. Lisa Grayshield and Ramon D. Castillo (Basingstoke: Springer Nature, 2020), 10. This is the description the authors provide of Indigenous Ways of Knowing.

5 Macarena Gomez-Barris, *Beyond the Pink Tide: Art and Political Undercurrents in the Americas* (Oakland: University of California Press, 2018), ebook.

6 José E. Muñoz, *Cruising Utopia: The Then and There of Queer Futurity* (New York: NYU Press, 2009), 1.

7 Mark Rifkin, *Beyond Settler Time: Temporal Sovereignty and Indigenous Self-Determination* (Durham, NC: Duke University Press, 2017), 2–3.

8 Kenny Ramos, 'Queer California: Untold Stories,' Oakland Museum of California, YouTube, November 4, 2019, https://www.youtube.com/watch?v=XOE5lvOXEGw

9 Arturo Escobar, *Pluriversal Politics: The Real and the Possible* (Durham, NC: Duke University Press Books, 2020), 7.

10 Asian Boss, 'Chinese React To Social Media Ban On Gay Content,' YouTube, last modified May 9, 2018, https://www.youtube.com/watch?v=sTzgE1nvxZs

Unbound is the world's first crowdfunding publisher, established in 2011.

We believe that wonderful things can happen when you clear a path for people who share a passion. That's why we've built a platform that brings together readers and authors to crowdfund books they believe in — and give fresh ideas that don't fit the traditional mould the chance they deserve.

This book is in your hands because readers made it possible. Everyone who pledged their support is listed below. Join them by visiting unbound.com and supporting a book today.

Anděla Bárová

Britney Bartz

Victoria Basug Slabinski

Noah Isaac Bateman

Baylee

Anuji Bedi

Sarah Beech

Sarah Beecham

Alyssa Beeker

Madison Bell

Sarah Bell

Dana Benelli

Louis Benzing

Elise Berendt

Catherine Berger

Chris Bergtholdt

Arun Berking

Sarah Berner

Julien Berra

Kaetlyn Bew

Susan Bittker

Alyx Bizel

Carolyn Black

BlushCW

Ceres Botkin

David J Bradley

Michelle Brady

Miranda Brewick

Emily Breyfogle

Emily Brightwell

Autumn Brooke

Jess Brooks

Brittainy Brown

Dwayne Brown

Julia Brown

Sam Buccino

Arly Buckinger

Kinga Budzyn

Emily Burgardt

Ashley Burgy

Nicole Burstein

Soraya Buschini

Arianna Bussoletti

Bee Buswell

Marissa Byfield

Pia C

Ida C.

Ares Cainzos

E Campbell

Eric Campbell

Bronwyn Cann

Zee Cannon

Bianca Caraza

Carla

Carlos

Katt Carlson

Sarah Carter

Carter

Krystle Castillo

August Blaine Centauri

Deborah Chalmers

Jessica Charles

Hana Chatani

Kerry Chin

Rebecca Chung
Katie Clark
Kerri Clark
Elizabeth Clarke
Catherine Clifford
Lindsey Cobb
Julia Cockman
Mara Coman
Vanessa Compagnoni
Anna C. Cook
Nick Cooper
Dan Corber
Chris Corby
Kimberly Cornelison
Coronatto
Tessa Corton
Kaitlyn Cottrell
Isabel Couchoud
Jules Coulter
Jenna Cowan
Bricke Crain
Kay Crawford
Lydia Creech
Crispyswift
Marion Cromb
Rachael Cronin
Marcus Cross
Natalie Cruz
Coke Cuadrado
Mona Cubells Escande
Kristin Cucolo
Harriet Cummings

Kotra D.
Halie Danielson
Alice Davis
Leigh Davis
Rosie Davis
Emory Daye
Stephanie De Brito Leal
Gerdien de Galan
Joanne Deeming
Ben Delahay
Nichole Elizabeth DeMeré
Jen Denison
Grant Denkinson
Shastra Deo
Rachael Dewhurst
Liz Dexter
Kane Dibb
Ash Dietrich
Alex Dillon
Mae Dingley
Harry Dixon
Sam Docteur
Claire Dore
Glen Downton
Asa Drake
Hannah Duncan
Avery Earle
Sarah Eccles
Maxine Eddy
M Edwards
Nadine Ehrhardt
Karina Eller

Ashley Elliott
Elm
Imogen Ely
Emily
Emma #FBPPR#NHS15
Ayelet Enisman
Kimm Eriksson
Marta Esteve
Vigdis Evang
Brookelyn Farrell
Hannah Fay
Sianna Ferguson
Marion Fetter
Aline Fierobe
Ralph Filthy
Matt Fishwick
Jessica Flake
Lucy Fletcher
Stephanie Flores
Thea Flurry
Vladimíra Fonfarova
Carter Ford
Clare Fowler
Foxintheteapot
Y Foy
Joel Francis
John Frewin
Katie Frey
L. L. Friedman
Divina Fuentes
Lee Fuller
Rai Furniss-Greasley

Ashley Gage
Azucena Juarez Galeas
Joël Galeran
Helen Gao
Kassandra Gardner
Surata Garratt
Jess Gates
F Gavin
Claire Genevieve
Rory Geoghegan
Katarzyna Gibson
Abigale Gigley
Olivia Giles
Rene Gilfillan
Nichola Giovanella
Clair Goff
Domonique Golden
Summer Gould
Laura Graham
Leah Westcott Graham
Benjamin Gray
JaLeisa Grayson
Ariel Grob
Julia Grosvenor
Dayna Groumoutis
RuthAnn Grumbling
Laura Guenzel
Larissa Guilford
Lindsey Gump
Erika Gundesen
Heather Gunson
Thomas Gurinskas

Johannes H.

Thadeus Hagan Smith

Garry Haining

Kathryn Haley-Halinski

Hallie Hamby

Bee Haralson

Sinead Harold

Emma Hartley

Laurie Hartley

Romy Harvey

Anne Hawley

Rhian Hay

Zachary Hayes

Sara-Jeanne Healey-Côté

Rachel Heath

Samuel Hedley

Kate Hemingway

Katherine Hempel

Jacqueline Henes

Anna Hepworth

Alison Herman

Nero Herrmann

Puck Heusinger

Lynn Heydasch

Rachel Hill

Ria Hill

Meredith Hilton

Rebecca Hindle

Chris Hitchcock

Amanda Jo Hobson

Emily Hodder

Emily Hogan

Selena Hogg

Rachel Holdforth

Paige Holland

Simchah Hollenbach

Camille Holmstedt

Michelle Hom

Michelle Hooks

Christy Houghton

Jay Humphrey

Rebecca Humphreys-Lamford

Mitchel Joffe Hunter

Sparrow Hurd

Alyx Hurst

Riam Hussain

Isabela Hutchings

Alina Ibach

Asma Ibrahim

Daniela Illing

Dizzy Inmotion

Juniper Page Irving

John Isaac

Spenser Isdahl

Jamie Jack

River Jackson

Sam Jackson

Stuart Jackson

Helena Jacobs

Sara Jaffer

S R Jakobi

Klára Janošková

Karolien Jaspers

Meghna Jayanth

Sadie Jeffries

Eli Jennings

Jin

Jessica Johns

Annika Johnson

Kim Johnson

Nicholas Johnson

Becky Johnston

Ellie Jones

Sophie Jones

Janelle Jordan

Mary Jordan-Smith

Joe Jukes

Laura Kajpust

Evan Kapros

Sparrow Kastelic

Hannah Kaye

Roz Kell

Rebecca Kendrick

Amber Keurhorst

Mia Khachidze

Imrose Khilji

Dan Kieran

Stephen Kilbride

Kay Kilfeather

Angela Kilian

Lovisa Kiltäpp

Harriet Kingsport

Noah Kleinn

Anna Kolber

Janet Kolsky

Claudia Kolts

Hayley Korczynski

Kathleen Kryger

Samantha Ksor

Anna Kurowicka

Claire Kuszynski

Annika Kwast

Jenn L

Rachel L.

Erin LaGrone

Tiffany Lam

Hannah Lamarre

Paige Landers

Mathilde Laniel

Camille Lapouge

Chris Lauretano

Jeremie Lauzon

Abigail Lawson

lazyfoxheart

Logan Lee

Margaret Lee

Rebecca Lee

Saturn Lee

Celeste Lee-Wo

Gilles Lefaucheux

Hannah Lenard

Sarah Lerner

Sarah Leveille

Maxine Levine

Bex Lewis

Dylan Lewis

Lida Lewis

Isabella Liberty

Pamela Lieber
Aroa Likona
Sarah Liles
Lillie (AliseOnLife)
Kelsey Joy Lindefjeld
Johanna Lindmark
Aleesha Linggi
Torie Linner
Hannah Lippard
Sarah Lister
Polina Litvak
Rachel Logan
Cruz Lopez
Sarah Lopez
Florïan Lorenzetta
Michelle Loseke
Katherine Lu
Claudia Luca
Samuel Ludford
Maria Lumbres
Lee M
MJ M
Alison Macdivitt
Lillian MacKnight
Sarah MacQueen
Susannah Maddock-Saint
Celia Magana
Méven Mahieux
Fiona Malpass
Mary March
Mareike
Jimmy Marsden

Alexis Marshall
Anna Martin
Ess L. Martinez
Jules Martinez
Walter Mastelaro Neto
Phoebe Mastrandreas
Chris Matthews-Darby
Brian Mattucci
Ruben Maurer
Shelby May
Morgan A. McFarland
Emily McGinty
Anthony Medina
Mohima Meera
Ry Megara
MegNot
Leslie Mei
Amy Meister
Marisol Mendez
Neil Meyer
Ashley Miller
John Mitchinson
Micah Mizukami
Kaycee Moore
Chai Morningstar-
    Abbernathy
Charlotte Morris
Seth Moulder
Autumn Mowrey
Morgen Mulcaster
Elizabeth Mundy
Giuliana Murekian

Abigail Murphy

Alison Murphy

Cara Murray

Lena Myers

Mo Nassar

Carlo Navato

Catherine Nel

Ether Nepenthes

Nerra

Candice Newton

Lexi Nguyen

Helena Nicholls

Clementine Noone

Beth Nuyens

Charly Nygaard

Charles Peter Nystrom

Ri O

Gwen O'Brien

Jenny O'Gorman

Ciara O'Shannessy

Glen Oakley

Anika Ochsenfahrt

Celeste Odell

OdinsSage OdinsSage

T. Odland

Mugren Ohaly

Jazmin Oliver

Zackery Olson

Kathryn Orr

Martina Orvošová

Joelle Owusu-Sekyere

Elk Paauw

Corinne Paben

Sam Pachico

Paula Page

Erin Partridge

Sawyer Patrick

Ruth Patten

Paupa

Jessica Pautler

Lucía Pavón Bejarano

Joanna Pearl

Lieselotte Peeters

Niki Pell

Ella Pendleton

Kerstin Penners

L Penny

Alexei Pepers

Matthew Peters

Emma H. Petersen

Elizabeth Petrichor

Petrichor

Lindsey Petrucci

Samantha Phelps

Gwendolyn Phillips

Olivia Phipps

Hannah Piekarz

Rowan Pierce

Paulina Piesik

Kiasha Pillay

Nivalis Plectrophenax

Esme Podmore

Dayvon Polite

Justin Pollard

Quinn Pollock
Polyanarchist
Kayla Ponder
Deepa Prasad
Halle Preneta
Megan Prime
Philip Pritchard
Annayah Prosser
Nat Przygoda
Laura Pugh
Will Purington
Queer Alliance Resource
    Center at UC Berkeley
Æmil Querre
C R
Francis R.
Haley R.
Daniel Rafferty
Kali Rainwater
Stephen Ralph
Evan Randolph
Sierra (TheGhostHybrid)
    Randolph
Rachel Ratzlaff Shriver
Felix Rauch
Dimitri Ray
Lee Raye
El Redman
Julia Reed
Rachel Reeves
MK Reibetanz
Yesenia Reveles

Charlotte Reynolds
Anassa Rhenisch
Lillie Rhodes
Kristina Richartz
Lexis Rivers
Roselle Roberts
Andrea Romero
Clara Romero
Jonathan Rose
Mara Rose
Joshua Rubino
Anna Sabiniarz
Daniela Sadło
Amanda Saffer
Betule Sairafi
Heidi Samuelson
Cynthia Santana
Wren Santiago
Henry Santos-Guzman
Sarah
Antoine Sarrazin
Daniel Satcher
Ceili Sauer
Sam Scala
Jay Scerba
Anne Schaefer
Caroline Schimkat
Karen Schipma
Sydney Schlenkermann
Melissa Schumacher
Bethany Schwartz
Ace Schwarz

Alexis Scott
Jonathan Scott
Lynsey Searle - Recommend
  Counselling
Angelina Seha
Rebecca Seibel
A.M. Sevin
Samantha Shannon
Laurence Shapiro
Bhagat Sharma
Jessica Shea
Jeffrey Shell
Anna Sherlock
Ricky Shields
Autumn Shuler
Louise Sidney
Silhouby
Selena Silva
Fraser Simons
Oliver Simpson
Rowan Singer
Jaye Smart
Markéta Šmídová
Bonnie Smith
Niall Snowden
Marcus Soll
Jonas Sollers
Kai Sorko
Lucia Soto-Hall
Martin South
Liam Southerland
Elizabeth Spencer

Frannie Sprouls
Kirsten Spryer
Wendy Staden
Alex Staehler
Clare Stark
Emily Starling
Katie Startup
Brianna Steelman
C. Steinegger
Anina Steinmann
Galaxy-Betsy Stovicek
Aimee Stubbs
Blair Subbaraman
Shelby Suderman
Katie Sumner
Sunshine
Scott Sutton
Benjamin T. R.
Anna-Theresa Taferner
Hiroshi Takai
Anne Tame
Jake Taylor
Scotty L Taylor
Rahini Thaker
Mei Theng Yew
Emma Thimbleby
Darwin Thomas
Cheyenne Thornton
Genevieve Ticknor
Kate Tilbury
Nicola Todd
Cristina Todea

Sabine Tötemeyer
Khoi Tran
Dave Treadwell
Magdalena Treutwein
Silke Troch
Meghan Tupper
Tasha Turner
D@lekc@tus Tweeticus
Martha Tyrrel
Tina Uhlmann
Fleur van Balen
Mick van de Loo
Luc van der Zandt
Zach Van Stanley
James Versace
VF
Giulia Viaggi
Jose Miguel Vicente Luna
Meera Vithlani
Kristīne Vītola
Johannes Vitzthum
Katie Volker
El Voss
@vronimus_ironimus@
    chaos.social
Doro W
Colleen Walsh

Rowan Walters-Brunt
Wardfire
Samantha Warren
Beth Weeks
Ray Westenberg
Sarah Wheatley
Miranda Whiting
Klara Widrig
Ell Williams
Freya Williams
Lauren Williams
Pip Williams
Rachael Williams
Kyra Wills-Umdenstock
David Wilson
Johanna Wilson
Beatrice Wing
Anna Wirtherle
Kayla Woodbury
Cheyenne Wray
Morgan Wright
Onir Ynao
PJ Young
Yulia
Ashley Zerne
Lisa Zillig
Zorume